Cooking Art

Cooking Art

Easy Edible Art for Young Children

By MaryAnn F. Kohl and Jean Potter

Illustrations by Ronni Roseman-Hall

gryphon house

Beltsville, Maryland

Dedication

To Larry Rood and Leah Curry-Rood, who have enriched my life

Mary Ann Kohl

To my Aunt Rosella and Uncle Mark Benish

Jean Potter

Acknowledgments

from Jean...
Thanks to Thomas, Archie and Shadow, my support team
Thanks also to Mary for her guidance

from MaryAnn...
Thanks in abundance to
Kathy Charner, for editorial magic and warm friendship
Michael Murphy, for sharing heaps of specialized, caring knowledge
Gryphon House, everyone, for support, good wishes and comfort in friendships
Michael, Megan and Hannah for everything

Cover Design: Graves Fowler Associates
Cover Photography: Straight Shots
Text Illustrations: Ronni Roseman-Hall

Library of Congress Cataloging-in-Publication Data

Kohl, Mary Ann F.
  Cooking art : easy edible art for young children
  Kohl and Jean Potter.
P. cm.
    Includes index.
    ISBN 0-87659-184-5
      1.   Cookery--Study and teaching. 2. Handicraft--Study and
teaching.   I. Potter, Jean, 1947-   .   II.   Title.
TX661.K65 1997
641.5'123--dc2l   97-8069
                                                     CIP

Table of Contents

Cooking Art

Using the Icons

On each recipe page of *Cooking Art*, icons are placed in the upper corner of the page to assist the cooking artists. Keep in mind that these categories are suggestions only. Many people enjoy breakfast foods at any time of the day, snack food for lunch or fruit and vegetables as an entree.

Ability level — indicates the ease or difficulty level of the cooking project for the child. All the projects are easy, but some are more time-consuming than others. These time-consuming projects require either an experienced helper or an experienced cooking artist. Even the most difficult projects are appropriate for beginning cooks, with a little extra supervision. Since cooking often requires the use of sharp, hot or other potentially dangerous materials, we assume that an adult will be helping with all cooking art projects.

    Easiest — good for beginning cooking artists

    Easier — good for cooking artists with a little bit of experience

    Easy — more challenging; requires an experienced helper

Preparation — indicates the approximate time an activity might take. Does not include set up time. Keep in mind that some children will speed through an activity, while others will take great care and time completing the same activity.

    This clock is the icon for preparation time. The following suggested time categories will be written below the icon:

10 to 15 minutes	15 to 30 minutes
about 30 minutes	about 45 minutes
1 hour or more	

    Bake — recipe requires an oven

Food Categories

 Beverage — a recipe to drink

 Bread — a bread dough or a recipe made with bread

 Breakfast — a recipe for food usually served at breakfast time

 Dessert — a recipe sweet in content

 Entree — a recipe that is appropriate as a main meal

 Fruit — a recipe that consists of fruits or a fruit salad

 Condiment or Garnish — a food to decorate or enhance the appearance or flavor of other recipes

 Pet Treat — recipe for pets, birds, critters, but not people

 Salad — a recipe consisting of foods in combination; it may include fruit, vegetable, meat or egg

 Sandwich — a combination of bread and a filling

 Soup — food eaten with a spoon appropriate for lunch, as an entree or a hearty snack

 Snack — food to eat between meals or as an appetizer

Vegetable — a recipe that consists of vegetables

Welcome

Cooking Art is a recipe book of creative, edible art experiences for children and adults. Cooking is an art, like painting, sculpting, acting, dancing or singing, and all of the arts thrive on experimenting, creating and exploring. Cooking artists can paint, draw, color and sculpt as they explore the tasty world of creative cooking and culinary design. The projects in *Cooking Art* allow children to discover the exciting art possibilities in food and to create art projects they can eat or serve to others. Using their own imaginations, children design food presentations or add creative finishing touches. They decorate cakes, sculpt with bread, paint with frosting, craft and design things for a gift or table decoration, build with fruit and much more. These art projects won't end up on the refrigerator door — they'll be in the refrigerator AND in someone's tummy! All of the food projects in *Cooking Art* are edible. No food is wasted or thrown away. *Cooking Art* encourages food design, not food play.

Cooking Art combines the familiar area of art exploration with the fascinating world of cooking and all its wondrous tools, tastes and outcomes. This book offers a wonderful opportunity for children to become comfortable and capable in the kitchen — with adult help and assistance — using exploration, discovery, creativity, and following simple directions to create uniquely designed, edible art. Each recipe allows ample room for cooking artists to explore and create in their own special, unique ways. The recipes in *Cooking Art* have lots of room for personal choices in foods selected, food design and food presentation. Although steps in the recipes should be followed, the outcome of each recipe can be completely different from one cooking artist to the next. The art process is of primary importance in *Cooking Art*. The product is the delicious reward for exploring the creative possibilities of cooking.

The kitchen is a place for meeting and learning, at home or at school — greeting and sharing comfortable times with family, friends, classmates and pets. The kitchen is also a learning laboratory and a studio for creative cooking artists to

✓ experience hands-on mathematics, like counting and measuring
✓ practice reading and comprehension
✓ discover the mysteries of chemistry
✓ build self-esteem by cooking useful, tasty products
✓ master manual dexterity
✓ create a delicious masterpiece

This book assumes that adults and children will work as partners. Take a little time before beginning, browse through this book and discuss and select recipes together. Agree on some simple rules to make the cooking experience smooth and successful. Remember to allow ample time to complete the recipes, as young children take longer to sift, stir and create than adults. Sometimes children simply love to knead and knead the bread or run the mixer just a little bit longer than necessary. So, work together — you may both come up with surprising and creative interpretations. Above all, remember: spills happen, patience is a virtue and not everything turns out as planned.

Enjoy the recipes, but most of all, enjoy cooking and learning (and tasting) together. Give the children room to be, to try and to...clean up!

Tips for Adults

Encourage children's natural creativity. Cooking together can be a memorable, delightful experience for both children and adults. To help the cooking experiences go well, the following considerations are a must:

✓ pay attention to preparation of materials and ingredients
✓ use caution and supervision with children of ALL ages.

The following suggestions will help assure successful creative exploration when preparing foods with children:

1. Read the recipe first. Determine if the recipe is appropriate for the child's ability level. Very young children may not enjoy recipes that require overnight freezing or complicated and lengthy instructions. Select recipes that can be completed within 15 or 30 minutes for younger children; older children can accept more waiting and detailed preparations.

2. Always use safety practices. When using a knife, be sure it is away from the child until it is to be used. When putting a pot on the stove, be sure handles are turned aside where they cannot be bumped. Always use a hot pad or oven mitt to handle hot baking sheets. Children must be supervised at ALL times.

3. Practice makes perfect. Before children use a knife or electric mixer or any other kitchen utensil, let them practice. A little practice will help prepare children to succeed without frustration or confusion.

4. Take time. Children do not work as quickly as adults. Be sure enough time is allotted to complete the recipe. General time guidelines are given for each recipe; however, you may want to allow additional time for collecting utensils and cleaning up.

5. Let children do the work. Children learn best by doing, so they need to be given the responsibility of doing the work. Assist them when they have difficulty with materials or tools, when they are handling sharp or hot materials or when something is too heavy. But for the most part, let them do as much as possible, even if they are making mistakes or learning as they go.

6. If possible, shop together. Some of the fun of preparation is shopping for the food and understanding where all this food comes from and how to get it ready. Shopping together also makes the recipe more special and fun. In addition, good discussion and teaching occurs when shopping in a store and selecting and comparing ingredients.

7. Clean up together. A child will learn to clean up properly and in an organized way if allowed to work alongside an adult. Children can be marvelously hard workers — especially when appreciated.

8. Enjoy! Take time to enjoy the fruits of your labor and share them with others.

Before Starting —
Things to Think About, Things to Know

1. Wash hands with soap and very warm water before beginning any project that involves food.

2. Wear an apron when cooking.

3. Read the entire recipe before starting any cooking project. This will help you decide if you like the recipe, where adult help is needed and if you have the proper equipment.

4. If unclear about cooking terms in the recipe, refer to the glossary in the back of the book.

5. Collect all of the ingredients and utensils listed in the recipe before beginning.

6. Place the ingredients and utensils on the work surface in the order in which they will be used.

7. If you have never used a certain cooking tool before, be sure to practice using it. Learn the correct and safe way to handle tools.

8. Follow one step at a time in the recipes. Don't skip a step or skip ahead in the recipe.

9. Measure the amounts needed in the recipe exactly.

10. Never allow any appliance or sharp tool to be used without adult supervision.

11. Always clean up when finished.

12. Share!

Chapter 1

Table & Kitchen

Monet

Handprint Apron

FABRIC PAINT

PLATES

SPOON

Materials

plastic sheeting
plain colored apron, one apron per artist
paper plates
fabric paints
spoons
paintbrushes
paper towels
permanent marker

Process

1. Cover the work area with the plastic.
2. Place an apron on the plastic, right side up.
3. Pour one color of fabric paint on each paper plate and spread the paint with a spoon. Use a different spoon for each color.
4. Use a paintbrush to paint the palm and fingers of one hand, covering the whole hand.
5. Press the painted hand onto the apron several times. It may be necessary to repaint the hand and fingers several times. If desired, rinse hands and use another color paint.
6. Wash and dry hands.
7. Allow the apron to dry for a day.
8. Use the permanent marker to decorate the dry apron by tracing handprints or writing names or words.
9. Wear the apron for cooking or art projects.

Printed Oven Mitt

Materials

fabric paints
paintbrush
baking sheet
plain colored oven mitt
black permanent marker
choice of kitchen tools for printing, such as

whisk	garlic press	wooden spoon
hand mixer	melon ball scoop	forks, spoons and knives

Process

1. Squirt colored puddles of fabric paint about 6 inches apart on a baking sheet, making sure the puddles do not touch. Set aside.
2. Select a kitchen tool.
3. Use the paintbrush to brush fabric paint onto the printing surface of the tool, and then press it on the oven mitt to make a print.
4. Repaint the tool and press it onto another space on the oven mitt.
5. Repeat this process with different colors (and different tools, if desired), covering one side of the mitt.
6. When this side is completely dry, turn the mitt over and print on the other side.
7. When both sides are completely dry, add more designs or outlines with a black permanent marker. Names, words or messages can also be written on the mitt.
8. Use this hand-decorated oven mitt when cooking, or hang the mitt on a hook in the kitchen to be enjoyed when not in use. This mitt is also a wonderful gift.

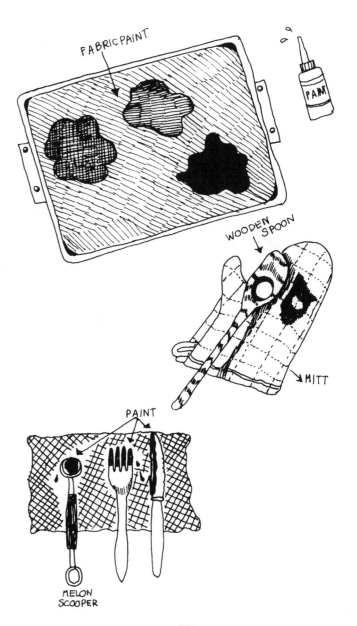

FABRIC PAINT

PAM

WOODEN SPOON

MITT

PAINT

MELON SCOOPER

Wooden Trivet

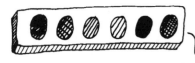
→ WATERCOLORS

Materials

block of wood (about 8"x 8" square & ½ -1" thick)
sandpaper
rag
paintbrush
watercolor paints
white glue
small felt scraps
jar of water
clear hobby coating (brush-on or spray)

Process

1. Sand the rough edges of a block of wood with sandpaper until smooth.
2. Dust away the sawdust with the rag.
3. Paint designs on the wood with watercolor paints and a paintbrush. Rinse the paintbrush out in water before using a different color. Let dry.
4. Turn the block of wood over.
5. Glue felt scraps on each corner of the block, or cover the entire back side with felt. Turn it back over so it is right side up.
6. Brush a clear hobby coating over the wood to protect the design and make it more water-proof. Let dry.
7. Use the decorated block as a trivet to protect the table from hot pots and dishes of food.
8. When not in use, the trivet makes a nice kitchen decoration on a shelf or in a windowsill.

Easy Table Cover

Materials

large piece of craft paper or butcher paper
scissors
peeled crayons
tape
items to use in creating crayon rubbings

yarn scraps	playing cards	scraps of heavy paper
doilies	coins	paper clips
leaves	metallic confetti	

other flat objects from around the house or outdoors

Process

1. Cover a table with a large sheet of craft paper or butcher paper.
2. Cut heavy scraps of paper into shapes, forms or figures with scissors.
3. Slip the heavy paper scrap shapes under the large butcher paper in a pattern or design.
4. Add other items under the butcher paper to create more shapes, patterns and designs.
5. Tape the butcher paper to the table to hold it in place.
6. Rub the paper with the sides of peeled crayons to reveal the hidden objects under the table covering. Feel with hands to discover any missed shapes or materials.
7. Rub and rub until the paper table cover is bright and festive. Remove tape.
8. Enjoy the table cover for a picnic, party or everyday use.

▲ Cut out shapes and designs with themes such as

dinosaurs	Christmas	insects
happiness	the environment	under the sea
recycling	travel	letters, numbers, shapes

easier   1 hour or more

Heirloom Tablecloth

→ PLACE MATS

Materials

plain white tablecloth or fabric (like a plain sheet)
cardboard rectangle the size of a place mat or a heavy plastic place mat
white chalk   white drawing paper, 11"x17"
fabric crayons   ironing board and iron
newsprint   fabric pens or permanent markers

Process

1. Spread the tablecloth out on the table. Using a crayon and a cardboard rectangle pattern or a thick plastic place mat, trace a place mat sized rectangle at each place where a family member sits.
2. Mark each family member's initial on the rectangle with white chalk which can be brushed away later.
3. Draw a design with fabric crayons on a sheet of drawing paper, one designed sheet of paper for each family member.
4. Next, place newsprint on the ironing board to protect the board, and then smooth out the tablecloth on the ironing board with the first of the family rectangles showing.
5. Place the first designed piece of paper face-down on the cloth in the chalked-in area for that family member.
6. Press a medium-hot iron straight down on the design and hold for several seconds, then lift the iron off the paper. Peek to see how the design is transferring from the paper to the cloth.
7. Repeat the pressing and ironing process until each design is completely transferred to the cloth.
8. Add names, messages or additional designs with a fabric pen or permanent marker by drawing or writing directly on the tablecloth, if desired.
9. Enjoy the tablecloth as a family heirloom for special occasions or for every day. Each child in a family may wish to create his or her own family heirloom tablecloth to keep forever, or each family member may wish to design his or her own place mat section.

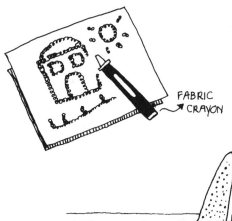

FABRIC
CRAYON

IRON

Natural Table Runner

Materials

needle and thread, pinking shears or sewing machine
flat, hard work surface such as a concrete floor
fresh leaves and flowers

scissors   unbleached muslin
grocery bags   table knife
hammer

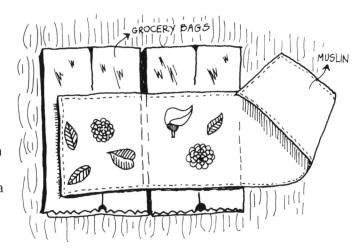

Process

1. Cut a piece of unbleached muslin fabric to measure about 2' wide by 5' long (or the length of the family dining table).
2. Turn the edges of the fabric down about ½ inch all the way around and sew in place with a sewing machine or by hand. Or, instead of sewing, the fabric could be cut with pinking shears or the edges left raw.
3. Spread the grocery bags out on a work surface such as a concrete floor that can take extreme pounding with a hammer.
4. Spread the fabric out on the grocery bags.
5. Arrange leaves and flowers on half of the fabric.
6. Fold the other half of the fabric over the arrangement. Do not place flowers and leaves on the fold.

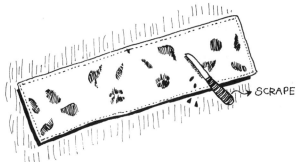

7. Next, feel where the leaves and flowers are with fingers to plan where to pound with the hammer. Pound on top of the leaves and flowers with the hammer until the juices and colors soak through the fabric.

▲ Only allow children who can handle a hammer properly to do this step. Supervise closely.

8. Open the fabric. Scrape away the plant residue with a fingernail or table knife. Spread the fabric on the table
9. Place a vase of flowers and leaves in the center of the table runner to complement the pattern. It looks nice to use the same variety of plants in the vase that were used to make the runner.

▲ The runner can be laundered, but will fade. Use cold water only. Do not use bleach.

Sewing Card Place Mats

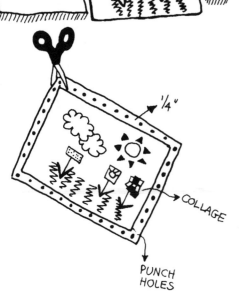

POSTER BOARD

¼"

COLLAGE

PUNCH HOLES

Materials

pencil
colored markers
ruler or spoon
toothpick
any tape

poster board in any color
rubber place mat to trace, optional
needle or pin
yarn

scissors
clear contact paper
hole punch

Process

1. With a pencil, trace or draw the shape of a place mat on the poster board. Cut out the poster board with scissors on the pencil line.

2. Create a design or picture on the place mat area with markers. Use other art techniques such as collage with wrapping paper or magazine pictures, fingerpainting, prints with kitchen utensils, crayon rubbings.

3. To protect the drawing and make the place mat more durable, cover both sides of the drawing with clear contact paper. Wrinkles and bubbles are common, though unappreciated. You can try rubbing them out with a ruler or the back of a spoon. Bubbles can be poked with a needle or pin and then rubbed out.

4. Cut around the edges of the place mat to trim uneven adhesive edges, but leave at least ¼ inch of the plastic adhesive as a border.

5. Rub the plastic all over (including the border area) with a finger, a ruler or the back of a spoon to force the plastic to stick to the drawing and also to make the picture show through more clearly.

6. Punch holes around the four edges of the place mat.

7. Tape one end of the yarn to an end of a toothpick, to be used as a needle. Sew the yarn through the holes, making any pattern. Add more yarn if needed. Keep the sewing a little loose so the mat stays flat. If the yarn is pulled too tightly, the mat will curl up. Sew or tie the end of the yarn around and around through the last two holes to finish.

8. Use the sewing card place mats for special occasions or everyday snacks. Wipe clean with a damp cloth or sponge. Do not soak with water.

Fancy Napkins

Materials

big bowl, bucket or sink
package of plain white handkerchiefs
nontoxic acrylic paint
plastic spoons
masking tape
towel or flat surface

a little liquid laundry soap
small paper cups
water
plastic sheeting
foam brushes in 1", 2" and 3" sizes

Process

1. Place the soap and warm water in a bowl, bucket or sink. Add handkerchiefs and let soak for a few minutes.
2. Take handkerchiefs out of the water and wring out. Spread each handkerchief out on a towel or flat surface and dry overnight.
3. The next day, squirt a different color of paint into each cup.
4. Add a few drops of water to smooth and thin the paint, using a separate spoon to mix each color. Mix paints together to create new colors, too.
5. Spread out the plastic sheeting on the floor or work surface as a protective covering.
6. Spread a handkerchief on the plastic. Tape the corners of the handkerchief to the plastic to hold it in place.
7. Paint designs on the fabric with foam brushes. Let dry.
8. When the handkerchiefs are dry, fold and use them as napkins.

▲ Fancy Napkins work well when used with Celebration Napkin Rings (page 20).

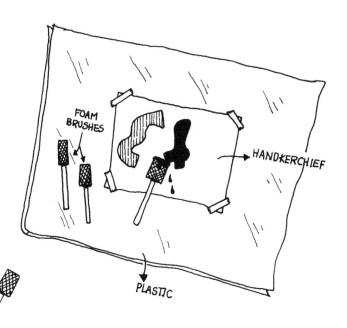

Celebration Napkin Rings

Materials

collect and save the plastic rings from empty cellophane tape rolls
bottles of nail polish, variety of colors
non-acetone nail polish remover (with adult help)
cotton balls or makeup pads for removal of spills, smudges
napkins (see page 19 for handmade napkin idea)

Process

1. Paint designs on the tape rings with the nail polish.
2. Let the nail polish dry overnight.
3. Roll, fold or stuff a napkin into each napkin ring to decorate a place setting for a special occasion.
▲ A variety of other art techniques can be used to decorate the napkin rings if nail polish is not handy or desired, such as
   ✓ paint napkin rings with any paints and then coat with clear gloss enamel when dry
   ✓ coat napkin rings with liquid starch and torn tissue pieces and then coat again, when dry, with clear gloss enamel
   ✓ decorate napkin rings with holiday symbols such as eggs, pumpkins, stars, bells or birthday cakes or
   ✓ spell out messages or names on the napkin rings.

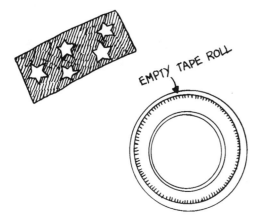

EMPTY TAPE ROLL

TISSUE PAPER

PUMPKINS

Natural Centerpiece

Materials

collect a variety of outdoor materials, such as
   pine cones, pine branches, magnolia leaves, berries
fruits or vegetables on hand, such as
   oranges, apples, bananas, grapes
large tray
large colorful ribbon
votive candle holders
votive candles

Process

1. Arrange the natural materials on the tray so they overlap one another and fill the tray.
2. Choose fruits and vegetables and place them among the natural materials on the tray.
3. Add a large ribbon to a corner of the arrangement to highlight the design.
4. Next, place votive candle holders in the arrangement (away from the ribbon for safety). Add votive candles to the candle holders.
5. Light the candles when the meal is ready to serve and enjoy the glowing beauty of the natural handmade centerpiece throughout the meal. Blow out the candles before leaving the table when the meal is over.

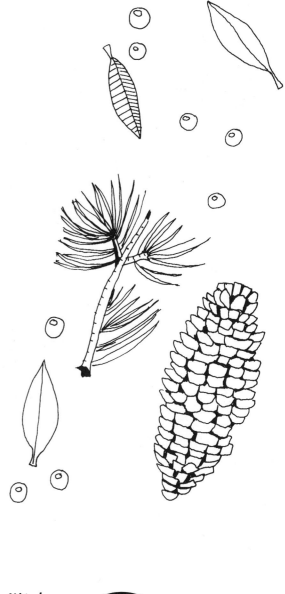

easy   about 45 minutes

Refrigerator Magnets

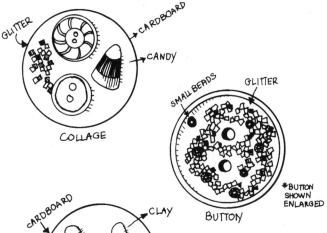

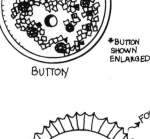

Materials

newspaper-covered work area
collect and assemble a variety of small collage items, such as
    small, bright candies, small buttons or beads, glitter
polymer modeling clay, such as
    Fimo

large buttons   small 1" circles of cardboard or heavy paper
strong hobby glue or tacky glue   small foil baking cups
clear craft or hobby coating (brush-on or spray)
round magnets, about 1" across or smaller (hobby or hardware stores)

Process

COLLAGE MAGNETS
1. Glue one or a few selected small collage items onto a cardboard circle. Dry briefly.
2. Glue a magnet on the back of the cardboard circle. Dry before using.

BUTTON MAGNETS
1. Glue beads and glitter on one side of a button. Dry briefly.
2. Glue a magnet on the other side of the button. Let dry. Brush with craft coating if desired.

CLAY MAGNETS
1. Form clay into little shapes or designs. Use as is or bake according to directions.
2. Glue the clay design or shape on one side of a cardboard circle. Dry briefly.
3. Glue a circle magnet to the other side. Dry before using.
▲ The magnet can be glued directly to the back of the clay design.

CANDY MAGNETS
1. Glue several little candies inside a small foil baking cup.
▲ Some candies will lose their color when varnished, so you may want to test a few before starting.
2. Coat with varnish. Dry for several days. Glue a magnet on the back of the foil baking cup. Dry before using. Magnet creations are great for holding a recipe card to a metal surface or decorating the refrigerator door.

With young children who still put things in their mouths, provide close supervision when the children are working with small materials.

Chapter 2

Shapes & Forms

easy | 1 hour or more | soup

Souper Noodles

Serves 10 to 15

Ingredients

2 to 2¼ cups sifted flour, plus extra

3 large eggs

1 pinch salt

2 large cans clear chicken broth

Utensils

2 bowls	measuring cups and spoons
fork	wooden spoon
rolling pin	pot
kitchen cloth	paring knife

Process

1. To make homemade shape-noodles, begin by mixing 2 cups of flour and a pinch of salt in a bowl. Set aside.
2. Crack the eggs into a separate bowl. Discard the shells. Lightly beat the eggs with a fork, then add to the bowl of flour and salt. Mix well with a wooden spoon.
3. When the flour mixture becomes too difficult to mix with the spoon, begin using hands and continue to mix. Work the flour mixture until it forms a ball of noodle dough.
4. Sprinkle several tablespoons of flour on the work surface and then place the noodle dough on the clean, floured work surface. Knead the noodle dough. If the dough is sticky, sprinkle with several tablespoons of flour. Knead the noodle dough until it is smooth and no longer sticky. Place the noodle dough into a bowl and cover with a cloth. Let stand for 30 minutes.
5. Divide the noodle dough into balls each about the size of an egg. Rub a rolling pin with flour and add a little more flour to the work surface. Roll the noodle dough balls on the work surface into ¼-inch thick sections of dough.
6. Use the point of the paring knife to make tiny cut shapes in the noodle dough sections. Score the shapes, then cut through the dough. See illustrations. Set noodles aside.
7. Pour the chicken broth into a pot. Place the soup on the stove and bring to a boil.
8. Add the shape-noodles to the soup. Simmer until the noodles are cooked — about 5 to 10 minutes.

Cooking Art

Chunky Square Kabobs

Ingredients

Serves 2 to 10

green, red and yellow peppers
cucumbers
zucchini
other vegetables, such as
    carrots, mushrooms, snow pea pods, olives
cubes of cheese, optional
any favorite recipe or ingredient for vegetable dip, such as
    salad dressing, honey and mustard, soft cheese spreads, herbed cottage cheese

Utensils

small bowls to hold vegetables, if needed
knife and cutting board
toothpicks
small dish for vegetable dip

Process

1. Remove the tops from the different kinds of peppers, then scrape out the seeds and the core by hand or with a knife.
2. Cut the peppers into squares about 1 inch in size. Cut the cucumber and zucchini into chunks.
3. Cut other vegetables of choice into chunks. Cheese cubes taste good and look colorful in kabobs too.
4. Assemble the chunks and squares of vegetables in any pattern on the toothpicks. Each kabob can be a different pattern. Kabobs can hold a single kind of vegetable, too, if desired. Be careful with the toothpicks; they can poke.
5. Place the dish of dip in the center of a serving plate. Arrange the kabobs around the dip.
6. Serve the kabobs as a party snack or an easy-to-eat salad with any meal.

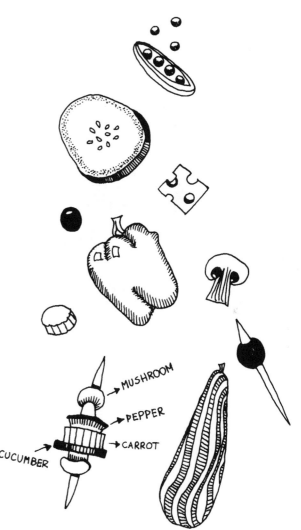

MUSHROOM
PEPPER
CARROT
CUCUMBER

Shapes & Forms

easy · about 30 minutes · bake · bread

Pain Décoré (French: Decorated Bread)

Serves 4 or more

GREASED COOKIE SHEET

Ingredients

frozen bread dough rolls (purchased bag of rolls, in balls)
beaten egg, in a cup
butter

Utensils

oven preheated to 350°F, or as directed on the frozen dough package

floured board	cookie sheet, coated with nonstick cooking spray
scissors	pastry brush
cup for egg	

Process

1. Thaw the frozen dough balls as directed on the bag, usually overnight.
2. To design the decorated French bread, think of shapes that use circles, such as a flower with petals or a bunch of grapes. For this project, a bunch of grapes will be described, but feel free to make up any designs, themes or shapes.
3. Place balls of dough on the greased cookie sheet in a grape pattern. See illustration.
4. Pull a ball of dough into a thick stem shape and tuck it into the top of the grape design.
5. Pull another ball of dough and roll into a vine. Arrange the vine across the balls of dough.
6. Let the dough rise for 30 to 60 minutes. Brush beaten egg on the grape design with the pastry brush.
7. Bake at 350°F for about 30 to 45 minutes, or as directed on the frozen bread dough bag. Remove the grape shaped bread when golden brown and hollow sounding when tapped with a knife handle.
8. Enjoy the Pain Décoré with butter, jam, honey or plain and warm from the oven. To eat, pull balls of baked bread from the larger grape design.
▲ Make decorated bread by forming letters, leaves, flowers, birds, fish or any other design from the dough before baking. Brush with beaten egg before baking.
▲ Note: Pain Décoré is pronounced pan day'-cor-ay'

Potato Ghosts

Four cups of potatoes serves 8

Ingredients

nonstick cooking spray
4 to 8 cups of any of the following mashed potatoes, such as
   1 package frozen mashed potatoes, fresh mashed potatoes, instant mashed potatoes
1 cup grated cheddar cheese
1 tablespoon butter or margarine
salt and pepper
6 tablespoons milk, plus extra
additional cold butter

Utensils

mixing spoon and bowl
oven mitt
large spoon
glass baking pan, microwave-safe
melon ball scoop

Process

1. Spray a light coating of cooking spray on a microwave-safe glass baking pan. Set aside.
2. Prepare the mashed potatoes. Make four to eight cups, depending on the hunger of those being served.
3. Add the cheese, butter, milk, salt and pepper to the potatoes and mix well. The mixture will be just right when it sticks together. If it is too dry, add more milk; if too moist, add a little flour.
4. Mold and moosh the potatoes into ghost shapes (or any other shape).
5. Set the potato ghosts and shapes in the baking pan and heat in the microwave on high for 2 minutes (or in a hot oven for 4 to 6 minutes). Remove the potato ghosts from the microwave. Be sure to wear oven mitts.
6. With a large spoon, transfer the potatoes from the pan to a serving plate.
7. Serve the potato ghosts with cold butter balls made with a melon ball scoop. Boo! Scary!

easiest   10 to 15 minutes   sandwich

All-a-Round Rice Cake

Allow 1 rice cake per person

Ingredients

large rice cake, one per person
peanut butter or other sandwich spread of choice
circle shaped foods, such as
    raisins
    sliced carrots
    sliced bananas
orange sliced in circles, to garnish

Utensils

spreading knife
knife and cutting board
paper doilies

RAISINS

CARROTS

PEANUT BUTTER

ORANGES

Process

1. Spread peanut butter on the rice cake with a knife.
2. Decorate the top of the rice cake circle with the circles of food, such as carrot circles, raisins or sliced bananas.
3. Make one rice cake for each person.
4. Place finished rice cakes on the round doily on a plate.
5. Garnish around the rice cakes with orange circles for a well-rounded lunch.

Circle Sandwich Cookies

sandwich

bake

about 30 minutes

easiest

Ingredients

bread slices, two per sandwich cookie
honey
melted butter
cup of soup per serving, optional

peanut butter
½ cup water in a cup
cold milk, optional

Utensils

oven preheated to 350°F
fork
baking sheet
choice of tools for cutting the bread into shapes, such as
    cookie cutters, any shape
    jar lids
    jars with medium-wide mouth
oven mitts

spreading knife
pastry brush
glass for milk or cup for soup, optional

Process

1. Use a cookie cutter, jar lid or wide jar mouth to cut shapes from the bread. Be sure to cut matching pairs of the shapes.
2. Spread one shape with peanut butter. Spread the matching shape with honey. Stick the two shapes together.
3. Dip the tines of the fork in water and press the tips of the tines around the edge of the sandwich to seal the peanut butter and honey inside. Press firmly, making little ½-inch lines around the edges of the sandwich.
4. Place the sandwich cookie on the baking sheet. Make as many sandwich cookies as desired, sealing each one and then placing it on the baking sheet.
5. When all the sandwich cookies are complete, brush the top of each one with melted butter.
6. Slip the sandwich cookies into the oven and bake at 350°F until toasty and brown. Wearing oven mitts, remove the sandwich cookies from the oven and cool slightly before serving.
7. Serve sandwich cookies slightly warm with a glass of cold milk and a cup of soup for a cozy lunch.
▲ On other occasions, experiment with sandwich fillings instead of peanut butter and honey, such as tuna salad, cheese, egg salad, taco meat, jelly or jam.

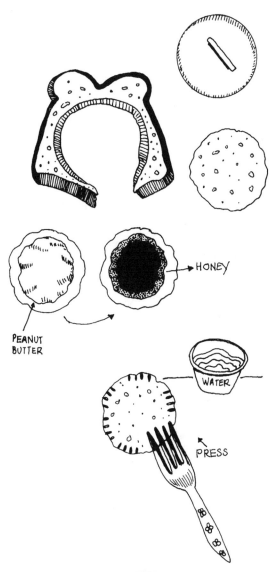

**Two slices of bread make
1 sandwich cookie**

HONEY

PEANUT BUTTER

WATER

PRESS

easy   about 30 minutes   sandwich

Pinwheel Sandwiches

Allow 1 to 3 rolled pieces of bread per person

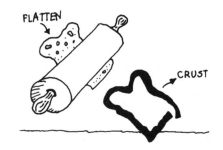

Ingredients

white slices of bread
variety of sandwich spreads, such as

tuna salad	egg salad	cheese spreads
peanut butter	chicken salad	cinnamon sugar
apple butter	jam	cream cheese

cheese
variety of fresh vegetable slices, such as

tomato slices	turnip slices	red, yellow and green pepper slices
carrot slices	celery slices	jicama slices
sliced mushrooms	sliced olives	

Utensils

knife and cutting board
rolling pin
spreading knife
toothpicks

Process

1. Cut the crusts off the slices of bread with a knife.
2. Flatten each slice of bread with a rolling pin.
3. Spread one tablespoon of sandwich spread on each slice of bread.
4. Starting with one side, roll the bread jelly-roll fashion. Secure with a toothpick.
5. Slice the roll into circles or pinwheels and put on a plate.
6. Cut the cheese into different shapes.
7. Cut the vegetables into shapes and slices.
8. Arrange the bread pinwheels, cheese shapes and vegetable shapes on serving plates in pinwheel or spinner designs, or in any other designs.

Meat Loaf Sculpture

Ingredients

Serves 4 to 6

1 stalk celery	1 small carrot	1 onion
2 eggs	1 cup oatmeal	1½ pounds ground beef
pinch of thyme	pinch of marjoram	½ cup ketchup
½ teaspoon Worcestershire sauce		

Utensils

oven preheated to 350°F	large mixing bowl
baking pan with sides	spatula
oven mitts	knife and cutting board

Process

1. Chop the celery, carrot and onion with a knife and put in a bowl.
2. Add the ground beef, eggs, oatmeal, thyme, marjoram, ketchup and Worcestershire sauce to the celery mixture. Mix the ingredients by hand, squeezing and working the meat mixture until well mixed.
3. Mold a ball of meat loaf mixture into several shapes or a large single shape to form a molded sculpture. Holiday shapes are especially fun and can make a holiday dinner more special. Hearts for Valentine's Day? Bats or ghosts for Halloween? A big shamrock for St. Patrick's Day?
4. Place the meat loaf sculptures in the baking pan and put in the oven. Bake for 1 hour or until well done.
5. Wearing oven mitts, remove the meat loaf sculptures from the oven. Let cool so the molded shapes will become more firm and hold together.
6. Carefully transfer the meat loaf sculpture with a spatula to a serving platter.
7. Arrange parsley and tomatoes around the meat loaf sculpture before serving.
8. Enjoy as the main course of a delicious, creative dinner.

▲ Tastes good served with Potato Ghosts (page 27).

Anna's & Lauren's Stomped Strawberry Shadow Sandwiches

Makes enough jam for a whole crowd — 2 slices of bread per person

Ingredients

8 cups fresh strawberries
½ teaspoon butter
7 cups sugar (or less, to taste)

jelling agent, such as Sure-Jell
loaf of favorite bread

Utensils

kitchen towels
hot soapy water
pot (large enough for child to stand inside with both feet)
5-quart pot
wooden mixing spoon
sterilized canning jars with lids
cookie cutters
spreading knife

Process

To make the fresh strawberry jam

1. Wash the strawberries and remove the stems. Place them in the large pot.
2. Spread kitchen towels on the floor. Place the pot of strawberries on the kitchen towels.
3. Meanwhile, wash feet well in hot soapy water and then dry with clean towels.
4. Step into the strawberry pot and gently stomp and crush the strawberries. Be sure to crush well by pressing down into them over and over.
5. When finished, step onto the kitchen towels and wipe feet well. Wash and dry feet (and hands) again before resuming the cooking project.

COOKIE CUTTER

6. Place the crushed strawberries in a 5-quart pot. Add the jelling agent to the strawberries, and then add the butter.

7. Place the pot of strawberries on the stove over medium high heat. Bring the mixture to a boil while stirring with a wooden spoon. Add the sugar to the strawberry mixture and continue stirring.

8. Remove the pot from the stove and then skim the foam off the top of the mixture with the spoon. Discard the foam.

9. Pour the mixture into the sterilized canning jars. Fill to $1/8$ inch from the top of the jar, then immediately screw the lids on tightly. Turn the canning jars upside down on the counter to cool.

To make the shadow sandwiches

1. While the jars cool, divide the bread into two equal piles.

2. Spread cooled strawberry jam mixture on each slice of bread from one pile. Set on a plate. From the other pile of bread, cut a shape with a cookie cutter into each slice of bread.

▲ A heart-shaped cookie cutter is nice for a Valentine celebration.

3. Make a shadow sandwich by putting one slice of strawberry-covered bread together with one bread cutout. The larger piece of bread will show around the cutout like a frame. Spread jam on cutouts, too, if desired.

4. Arrange the shadow sandwiches on a plate for a fresh strawberry treat.

▲ Extra strawberry jam should be stored in the refrigerator or frozen.

This recipe was contributed by Bob Passarelli, Chef, Governor's Executive Mansion, Raleigh, North Carolina.
His daughters, Anna and Lauren, enjoy assisting their dad in the kitchen.

Popcorn Sculpting

Serves 4 to 8

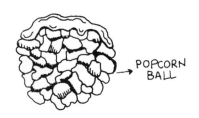

→ POPCORN BALL

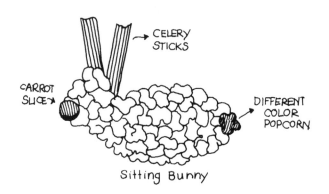

CELERY STICKS

CARROT SLICE

DIFFERENT COLOR POPCORN

Sitting Bunny

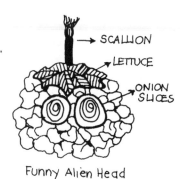

→ SCALLION

→ LETTUCE

→ ONION SLICES

Funny Alien Head

Ingredients

¼ cup margarine, plus 1 tablespoon extra

1 bag mini-marshmallows

12 cups popped popcorn

3 packages gelatin (such as Jell-O, 4 serving size), different flavors and colors

choice of the following foods, such as

| shredded lettuce | bran sprouts | onion rings |
| scallions | celery sticks | carrot slices |

Utensils

3 bowls

oven mitts

wax paper

large wooden spoon

large microwave-safe bowl or saucepan

Process

1. Place the margarine and the marshmallows in the microwave-safe bowl.
2. Microwave the margarine and marshmallows on high 1½ to 2 minutes (or melt on top of the stove in a saucepan for 3 to 4 minutes) until the marshmallows are puffed.
3. Remove the bowl of marshmallows from the microwave. Wear oven mitts. Stir the marsh-mallow mixture with a wooden spoon.
4. Divide the popcorn equally into three separate bowls.
5. Pour equal amounts of the marshmallow mixture over popcorn.
6. Sprinkle a different color of gelatin over each bowl of popcorn and marshmallow mixture. Quickly stir with a spoon until the gelatin and marshmallow mixture evenly covers the pop-corn mixture.
7. Let the marshmallow and popcorn mixture cool slightly.
8. Rub some margarine on both hands. Take some of the popcorn mixture and mold into an interesting form. Add different colors of the popcorn mixture to make parts of the sculpture.
9. Place the sculpture on wax paper on a serving plate. Add any of the remaining foods to make an interesting presentation of the sculpture just before serving.

Delicate Triangle Tea

snack

about 30 minutes

easy

Ingredients

sliced bread

jelly, jam or fruit preserves, optional

tea bags

butter, margarine or cream cheese

colored sugar sprinkles, optional

boiling water in a kettle on the stove

**Allow 4 triangles (1 slice of bread)
per person**

Utensils

knife and cutting board

pretty plate and fancy napkins, optional

vase and flower, optional

spoon

tea cups and saucers

teapot

Process

1. Decide how many sandwiches to make. One slice of bread per person is usually about right, but make extras just in case.
2. Trim the crust from the bread slices with the knife.
3. Cut the bread corner to corner, forming triangles.
4. Spread each triangle with butter, margarine or cream cheese.
▲ Butter, margarine or cream cheese may be colored with food coloring before spreading on the triangles.
5. Add dots or small puddles of jam to the spread on each triangle, if desired. Lightly sprinkle each triangle with colored sugar sprinkles, or think of other ways to decorate the delicate triangles.
6. Boil the water and make the tea.
7. Pour the tea into cups and arrange on the table. Fancy napkins or a pretty flower in a crystal vase will add to the teatime mood.
8. Serve the triangles on a pretty plate to enjoy with a lovely cup of tea.

Shapes & Forms

Beloved Strawberry Hearts

Serves 4 or more

Ingredients

frozen pint of strawberries

heavy cream

pint of fresh strawberries

vanilla or strawberry ice cream, optional

Utensils

individual white dessert plates, one for each beloved person

knife and cutting board

cup

toothpick

scissors, optional

blender

eyedropper

ice-cream scoop, optional

Process

1. Thaw the box of strawberries slightly by letting it sit on the counter for 30 minutes. Meanwhile, wash and drain the fresh strawberries.
2. Cut the fresh strawberries in half with a knife from stem to point to resemble hearts. Set aside.
3. Open the slightly thawed box of strawberries. Put the strawberries in a blender. Blend until smooth.
4. Spoon the blended strawberry sauce on individual white dessert plates, covering and filling the bottom of the plate with a thin layer of strawberry sauce.
5. Next, pour the heavy cream into a cup. With an eyedropper, squeeze and drop small dots of cream in different places in the strawberry sauce on each plate.
6. Stick the point of a toothpick in the center of a cream dot and drag it through the dot to create a heart design. This will take very little practice. Repeat this procedure until all of the dots of choice have become hearts. Some dots can be left as dots.
7. Place the drained and cut fresh strawberry halves in any design throughout the strawberry sauce and cream hearts.
8. Add a scoop of strawberry or vanilla ice cream to the dessert, if desired.
9. Serve the individual desserts immediately. For optional table decor, cover the table with a white tablecloth and accent with red napkins, doilies, a flower arrangement of roses or red tulips, confetti or hearts cut from paper.

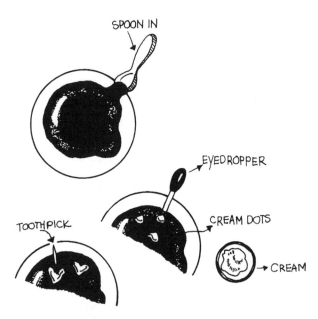

SPOON IN

EYEDROPPER

CREAM DOTS

TOOTHPICK

CREAM

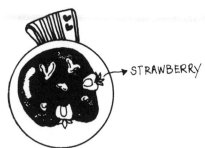

STRAWBERRY

Chapter 3

Color & Design

Lemon Lights

Serves 6 to 8 thirsty cooking artists

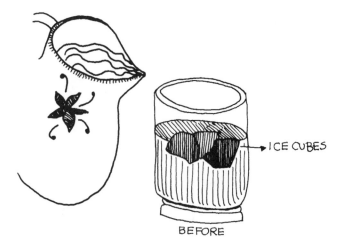

→ ICE CUBES

BEFORE

AFTER

Ingredients

purple grape juice
lemonade from mix, frozen concentrate or fresh-squeezed

Utensils

pitcher
ice cube trays
glasses

Process

1. Pour the grape juice into the pitcher.
2. Fill each compartment of the ice cube trays with grape juice.
3. Place the ice cube trays in the freezer and freeze overnight.
4. The next day, prepare the lemonade in the pitcher.
5. Remove the ice cubes from the freezer. Take the ice cubes out of the tray.
6. Place several ice cubes in each glass. Pour lemonade over the ice cubes.
7. While drinking watch what happens to the colors in the lemonade.

Kaleidoscope Salad Plate

salad

about 30 minutes

easier

Ingredients

Serves 4 or more

fresh vegetables, such as
  firm tomato, carrot, celery
fresh or dried herbs, such as
  parsley, mint, celery leaves
fresh greens, such as
  lettuce, spinach, kale
optional foods, such as
  cheese slices, cold cuts
light vinegar and oil salad dressing

Utensils

kaleidoscope
cutting board and paring knife
clear glass plate or platter

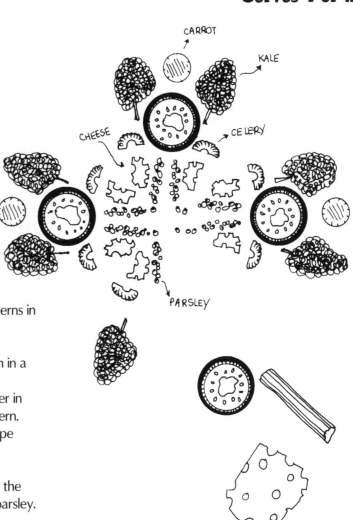

Process

1. Look through a kaleidoscope to see the designs made inside. Notice the repeated patterns in the circular design. The repeating circle will be a theme in the salad recipe.
2. Slice the tomato into very thin slices.
3. Place the tomato slices on the clear glass platter in a circular design, similar to a pattern in a kaleidoscope.
4. Slice or tear an herb or green food into pieces. The pieces should resemble one another in size and shape. Add these herb pieces to the design, continuing the kaleidoscope pattern.
5. Add more slices, pieces and shapes of foods and place them in the circular kaleidoscope design on the plate.
6. Sprinkle the platter of vegetables with the light salad dressing. Chill for ½ hour.
7. To serve, place the platter on a table and eat parts and pieces of the pattern, keeping the design intact as long as possible. For example, eat all the tomatoes first. Next eat the parsley. Watch the design become less crowded while still maintaining a kaleidoscope look.
▲ As an optional idea, place the platter on a glass table, lie down under the table, and look at the design through the table and through the platter. A bright light or sunny day will help the design look more like a kaleidoscope. Also, this recipe makes an attractive party salad.

Easy Swizzle Sticks

Serves 10 to 15

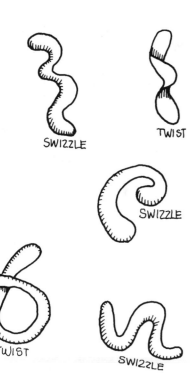

SWIZZLE

TWIST

SWIZZLE

TWIST

SWIZZLE

TWIST & SWIZZLE

SWIZZLE

Ingredients

nonstick cooking spray
2 tablespoons butter, melted
1 teaspoon poppy seeds
dip for bread, such as
    peanut butter   herbed butter
    honey mustard   other sandwich spreads

2 cans refrigerated soft bread sticks
1 teaspoon sesame seeds

Utensils

oven preheated to 350°F
2 baking sheets
pastry brush
spatula
oven mitt
cup

Process

1. Spray a light coating of cooking spray on the baking sheets.
2. Open the package of refrigerated bread sticks and separate into strips.
3. Make each dough strip into a design. Twist or swizzle the breadsticks making each one different. See illustration.
4. Place the dough strip designs 2 inches apart on a baking sheet.
5. Brush dough strips with butter and sprinkle with seeds.
6. Place the dough designs in the oven for 15 minutes or until golden. Wear an oven mitt to remove the bread from the oven.
7. Let the bread cool for a few minutes, then remove the bread designs from the pan with the spatula.
8. Arrange the bread designs on the platter so all the designs show. Place the dip in a cup on the platter. Serve as part of a meal, such as with soup or salad.

Polka Dot Party Melon

fruit

about 30 minutes

easier

Ingredients

Serves 8 to 12

2 melons of contrasting colors, such as
   cantaloupe and honeydew
additional selection of fruits cut with a melon ball scoop, or circle-shaped fruits, such as

apple balls	kiwi balls	raspberries
peach balls	red grapes	blueberries
green grapes	banana balls	strawberries

Utensils

knife and cutting board	hand towel
small melon ball scoop	2 bowls (or more if needed)
2 large plates or platters	spatula

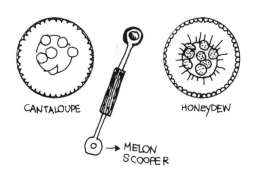

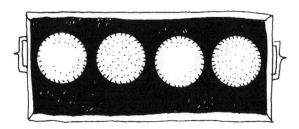

Process

1. Slice two melons of contrasting inside color in half. Scoop out and discard the seeds and pulp. Cut away the skin from all four halves and discard. Dry hands on the hand towel as needed to prevent slippery hands.
2. Place two melon halves of contrasting colors (like honeydew and cantaloupe) upside down like domes on one large platter. Place the other two melon halves on the other platter, also like domes. (Place all four halves on one platter if the platter is large enough.)
3. Scoop one ball from the orange cantaloupe and place it in a bowl. Scoop one ball from a green honeydew and place it in the other bowl. Continue scooping balls from both halves and placing the balls in the bowls. Make a design or pattern of holes in the melon halves, if desired. Work carefully, keeping the melon halves intact.
4. When the halves are filled with holes, begin making the polka dot design. Take an orange melon ball and place it in a hole in the green melon. Then, take a green melon ball and place it in a hole in the orange melon. Fill all the holes with contrasting melon colors.
5. Scoop balls from other fruits and plug them into the melon holes too, if desired. Some fruits like raspberries or grapes may fit right into the holes.
6. When all the holes are filled, follow the same procedure with the other two melon halves. Add optional fruit balls or circle shaped fruits, if desired.
7. Serve the polka dot melons on platters for a cheerful, festive party snack. Guests can slice through the melon domes and serve themselves with a spatula on salad plates.

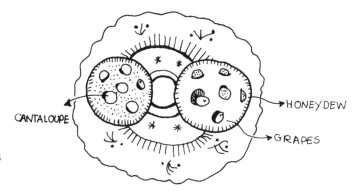

Color & Design

easier   about 45 minutes   fruit

Etched Melon Bowl

Serves 2 to 6

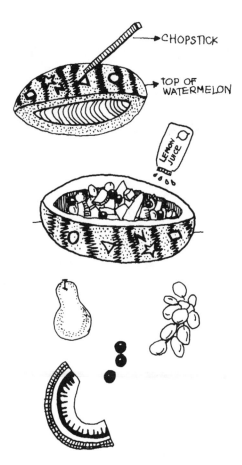

CHOPSTICK

TOP OF WATERMELON

LEMON JUICE

Ingredients

watermelon
variety of melons, such as

| cantaloupe | honeydew | crenshaw |

variety of fresh fruits, such as

| strawberries | blueberries | grapes |
| peaches | pears | pineapple chunks |

lemon juice

Utensils

knife and cutting board   clear plastic wrap
small bowls or mixing bowls   towel for slippery hands
chop stick, melon ball scoop or other kitchen tools for scraping, cutting

Process

1. Cut the watermelon in half with a knife. Wrap one-half of the watermelon with clear plastic wrap and put in the refrigerator for a later recipe or snack.
2. Scoop all the pulp and seeds (if any) from inside the other watermelon half. Scrape out the pink watermelon meat, place it in a bowl and set aside.
▲ Be careful with this next step as hands can be slippery. Use a towel to dry hands if needed.
3. Place watermelon half upside down, like a dome, on work surface. With the point of a chop stick or the edge of a melon ball scoop, etch and scratch designs, shapes, numbers or letters through the outer layer only of the green watermelon skin. Try not to cut a hole completely through the skin. Place the empty watermelon bowl on a platter.
4. Cut the other fruit in half. Scoop out the seeds and pulp from inside the melon halves. Cut away the skins of the melons. Slice the melons into sections. Cut the melons and other fruits into different shapes with a knife or scoop.
5. Now fill the watermelon bowl with the fruit shapes and other smaller fruits. Sprinkle lemon juice over all the fruits in the bowl and mix gently.
6. Arrange cut-up fruits around the base of the melon bowl to garnish, and add a serving spoon and small dishes to serve. Enjoy the etched watermelon bowl and fresh fruit as a colorful healthy snack, refreshing salad or light lunch.

Mush & Jelly Paint

Ingredients

Allow 1 bowl per person

smooth jelly
hot cereal, such as Cream of Wheat
fresh or canned fruits of choice, such as

banana circles	peaches	strawberries, whole or slices
berries	pears	raisins

brown sugar and milk, optional

Utensils

clean squeeze container such as mustard comes in
saucepan
mixing and serving spoon
bowls for fruit

Process

1. Fill the clean squeeze container with jelly. Fill several containers with different jelly flavors, if desired. Set aside.
2. Prepare the cereal on the stove in a saucepan according to box directions. Most hot cereals take 10 minutes or less.
3. Spoon the warm, cooked cereal into serving bowls.
4. Serve each person a bowl of cereal. Each person can draw pictures and designs by squeezing the jelly onto the cereal.
5. Add designs and decorations with fruits of choice, such as banana circles or strawberry slices.
6. Serve with brown sugar and milk, if desired. Enjoy as a hearty, colorful breakfast.

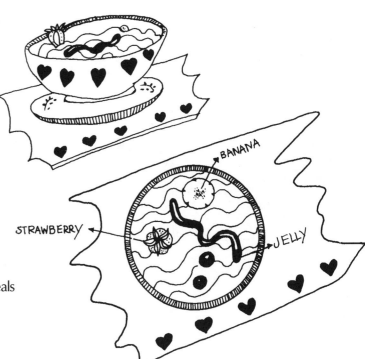

Snow White Snowflake

Allow 1 tortilla per person

MOZZARELLA CHEESE

TORTILLA

Ingredients

package of flour tortillas
shredded mozzarella cheese (or any white cheese such as Monterey Jack
　　or natural, white cheddar)

Utensils

kitchen scissors
baking sheet
oven mitts
spatula

Process

1. Fold the tortilla in half and then in half again. Hold the folds together.
2. Cut out shapes and designs from the folded edges of the tortilla with the kitchen scissors. Cut through all of the layers, trying not to tear the tortilla.
3. Open the tortilla and place it flat on the baking sheet. It should resemble a snowflake design. If more design is desired, refold the tortilla and add more cuts and holes. Place on the baking sheet.
4. Carefully sprinkle the shredded mozzarella cheese on the snowflake tortilla. Try to keep the cheese on the tortilla and not in the holes.
5. Place the baking sheet and snowflakes under the broiler just until the cheese bubbles. Watch carefully — it only takes a few seconds. Wearing oven mitts, remove the baking sheet from the oven. Set aside and let cool for a few minutes.
6. While waiting, sprinkle a little cheese on the white plate.
7. Then, with a spatula, remove the tortilla snowflake from the baking sheet.
8. To serve, place the tortilla on a white plate. Sprinkle with a little more cheese, if desired.

Tiny Trifles

Ingredients

6 to 12 prebaked cupcakes, any flavor

choice of nonfat yogurt in three flavors, such as
vanilla, strawberry, lemon

choice of fruit in different colors, such as
raspberries, blueberries, strawberries, grapes

mint sprigs, optional

Allow 1 trifle per person

Utensils

knife and cutting board

spoons

wide mouth glasses, one for each cupcake

spoon

ice tea spoons

YOGURT ON SIDES

YOGURT

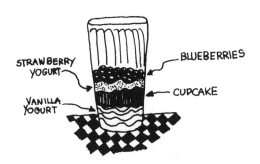

STRAWBERRY YOGURT

BLUEBERRIES

VANILLA YOGURT

CUPCAKE

Process

1. Slice one cupcake into three layers. Set aside.
2. Place several spoons of one flavor of yogurt in a glass. Be sure to completely cover the bottom of the glass with the yogurt. Spread a little of the yogurt up the sides of the glass too.
3. Place a slice of cupcake on top of the yogurt.
4. Add another color of yogurt on top of the cupcake slice.
5. Arrange some fruit on the yogurt. When arranging the fruit pieces, hold the glass up and note the way they look from outside the glass. Press some against the sides of the glass.
6. Continue to layer the cupcake slices, yogurt and fruit pieces.
7. Top off the cupcake with a piece or two of fruit and a sprig of mint to decorate.
8. Place the tiny trifles in the refrigerator for about 1 hour to chill.
9. Serve with an ice tea spoon for a colorful trifle dessert experience.

easiest   about 45 minutes   dessert

Frozen Color Pops

Each paper cup makes 1 juice pop

Ingredients

½ cup orange juice
1 teaspoon sugar
¼ cup grape juice

3 ounces fresh raspberries or strawberries
¼ cup cold water
¼ cup water

Utensils

4 small paper cups   blender
strainer   measuring cups
ice-cream sticks or craft sticks

Process

1. Pour about 1 inch of orange juice into each paper cup.
2. Place the cups in the freezer for about 2 hours.
3. Place the raspberries or strawberries, sugar and water into the blender and process until smooth.
4. Pour this berry mixture through a strainer. Set aside.
5. Remove the frozen orange juice from the freezer. Pour the strained berry mixture over the frozen orange juice.
6. Return the frozen juices to the freezer for about 1 hour, until almost frozen.
7. Mix grape juice with ¼ cup cold water. Set aside.
8. Remove the frozen orange juice and berry mixture from the freezer. Pour the grape juice mixture over strawberry or raspberry layer. Insert ice-cream sticks or craft sticks and freeze the mixture overnight.
9. Take the fruit pops out of the freezer and let sit for a few seconds, then grasp by the handles and pull the pops out of the cups to eat. Notice the variations of colors in the layers of frozen pops.

Rainbow Snow Slushies

dessert

about 45 minutes

easiest

Ingredients

crushed or shaved ice to fill 2 tall glasses
2 cups milk or cream
optional flavor, colors or foods, such as
food coloring, banana, fruit juices, berries

¼ teaspoon vanilla
2 tablespoons sugar

Serves 2 — or recipe can be doubled, tripled or quadrupled for as many people as there are glasses to fill

Utensils

2 clean towels and hammer (or ice crusher)
measuring cups and spoons
tall, large glasses
white paper and scissors, optional

mixing bowl
blender, fork or whisk
long spoons

Process

1. Place ice cubes between two clean towels and hammer until crushed, or use the ice crusher. Place in the mixing bowl.
2. Add 2 cups of milk or cream to the bowl. Then, add ¼ teaspoon vanilla and 2 tablespoons sugar. Mix well with a whisk or fork.
3. Pour the sweetened ice in a blender and blend until slushy and smooth.
▲ If there is no blender handy, use a fork or whisk to beat to a slushy mixture.
4. If desired, blend in any food color, fruit or fruit juice for additional flavor and color.
5. Pour the Snow Slushies into 2 tall glasses. It's fun to make several different colors of Snow Slushies, and then scoop or layer them into tall glasses in rainbow stripes. Layers of different flavors are fun to eat.
6. To garnish the tall glasses in a wintry way, serve the Snow Slushies on coasters or doilies made by hand. Make doilies by cutting white paper into at least one snowflake for each person, using the following directions or in any other imaginative way.
7. Fold white paper in any fashion, such as in squares. Cut on the folds, removing large or small pieces of paper and leaving holes. Open the folded paper and a freehand, simple "snowflake" will remain.
8. Eat the slushies with long spoons.

Mosaic Pie

Serves 6 to 8

Ingredients

1 box vanilla instant pudding mix
4 cups strawberry frozen yogurt or ice cream
¾ cup skim milk
prebaked graham cracker pie crust
any variety of favorite fruits in pieces, slices and chunks, such as

strawberries	blueberries	oranges
peaches	star fruit	papaya
bananas	pineapple	kiwi fruit

Utensils

mixing bowl
electric mixer
knife and cutting board
spatula

Process

1. Place the pudding mix, frozen yogurt and milk in the mixing bowl.
2. Beat the ingredients with the electric mixer until smooth and thoroughly mixed.
3. Pour the pudding mixture into the graham cracker pie crust.
4. Create a mosaic design on top of the pudding pie with selections of favorite fruits. Fill the entire pie's surface so that very little of the pudding mixture shows through. Create flowers, faces, birds, geometric designs or other mosaic designs or shapes.
5. Place the mosaic pie in the refrigerator until cold and firm, at least one hour.
6. Take the mosaic pie out of the refrigerator when it is firm.
7. Cut the pie with a knife and slip each piece of pie onto a plate to serve.
8. Decorate around the slice of pie with extra bits and pieces of fruit.

Chapter 4

Numbers & Letters

Number Pretzels

Serves 10 to 15

Ingredients

1½ cups warm water
1 teaspoon salt
1 beaten egg

1 teaspoon sugar
1 package yeast
1 tablespoon water

nonstick cooking spray
4 cups sifted flour, plus extra
coarse or regular salt, optional

Utensils

baking sheet
spoon
spatula

mixing bowls
oven mitt
knife

pastry brush
mixing spoon
oven preheated to 350°F

Process

1. Spray a light coating of cooking spray on the baking sheet.
2. Place the warm water in a mixing bowl. Add the sugar and salt to the warm water. Sprinkle the yeast on the water and mix slowly until dissolved. Add the flour to the yeast mixture and mix well with hands.
3. Sprinkle 2 tablespoons flour on the work surface. Place the flour mixture on the work surface and knead until it is a smooth, elastic dough. Add a bit more flour to prevent sticking, if necessary.
4. Roll out the dough by hand into a long rope or snake, then cut the dough into strips with a knife. Roll these strips by hand into ropes, and shape them into numerals. Place them on the baking sheet.
5. Crack the eggshell against the side of a bowl, breaking open the egg and letting it fall into the bowl. Discard the broken shell.
6. Add 1 tablespoon water to the egg and whisk until mixed. Brush each numeral with a pastry brush dipped in the beaten egg. Then, sprinkle the pretzels with salt, if desired.
7. Place the baking sheet in the oven and bake for 15 minutes. Wear an oven mitt and remove the baking sheet from the oven. Let cool.
8. Remove the baked numeral pretzels from the baking sheet with a spatula.
9. Serve as part of a meal, as an appetizer or as a warm snack. Delicious with soup!
▲ This pretzel recipe works for any design, such as animals, letters, bugs, flowers or freeform shapes of any kind. Pretzel shapes are fun, too.

Cinnamon Letters

bread bake 1 hour or more easier

Ingredients

Serves 4 to 8

1 package of frozen bread dough rolls
2 teaspoons flour
2 teaspoons water
2 teaspoons cinnamon

nonstick cooking spray
1 egg
½ cup granulated sugar

Utensils

oven preheated to 400°F

baking sheet   2 mixing bowls   whisk
pastry brush   oven mitt   spatula

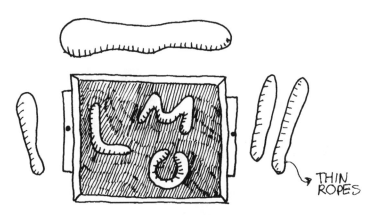

THIN ROPES

Process

1. Open the package of frozen dough and let it thaw on a clean work surface.
2. Spray a light coating of cooking spray on the baking sheet. Set aside.
3. Sprinkle 2 teaspoons of flour on the work surface. Roll each dough ball into a rope about 18 inches long. Cut the ropes into three shorter ropes about 5 to 6 inches long each. Place the shortened ropes on the baking sheet. Form letters with the ropes of dough.
4. Now, place the baking sheet in a warm place for 30 minutes to let the dough rise.
5. While waiting, crack open the egg. Separate the egg white and yolk. Place the yolk in another bowl to save for another recipe. Add the water to the egg white and whisk until fully mixed.
6. When the dough has risen for 30 minutes, brush the egg white mixture on each letter for a shiny glaze.
7. In a second bowl, combine sugar and cinnamon. Sprinkle the cinnamon sugar on the letters.
8. Place the baking sheet in the oven and bake for 15 to 20 minutes or until golden brown. Wear an oven mitt and remove the baking sheet from the oven to cool in a safe place.
9. When cool remove the bread dough letters from the baking sheet with a spatula.
10. Arrange the letters on a serving tray. Letters can be arranged to spell words, initials of friends or in any pattern or design.
11. Eat the sweet letters as a snack, dessert or party treat.

SUGAR + CINNAMON

SPRINKLE LETTERS

Fruit Spellers

Serves 2 or more

Ingredients

any choice of fruits, such as

cantaloupe   honey dew   kiwi fruit

berries   apples

mangoes

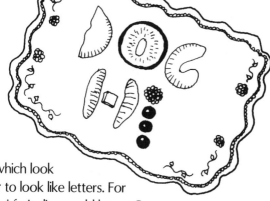

Utensils

knife and cutting board
kitchen scissors

Process

1. Peel the skins off all of the fruits.
2. Cut the fruits with a knife into ¼-inch slices.
3. Place the fruits on a serving tray.
4. Study the shapes of the fruits to determine which look like letters and which can be placed together to look like letters. For example a melon slice could be a U and a kiwi fruit slice could be an O.
5. Arrange letters on the serving plates to spell words or write initials.
6. Fruits may be cut or enhanced to form letter shapes with kitchen scissors or a knife, if desired. Smaller fruits, like blueberries and raspberries, can be lined up to form letters or spell words or names.

MANGO

KIWI

HONEY DEW MELON

Number Skewers

fruit

about 30 minutes

easiest

Ingredients

cantaloupe or honeydew melon
yogurt, optional
honey, optional

Utensils

knife and cutting board
number cookie cutters or sharp knife
melon ball scoop
bowl
wooden skewers
small bowl for dip, optional

Process

1. Cut the melon in half. Clean the seeds out of the melon. Cut the skin off the melon.
2. Cut only one-half of the melon into slices about ¼- to ½-inch thick. Place the melon slices on their sides.
3. Press the number cookie cutters (or sharp knife) into the melon slices to make numbers.
4. Use the melon ball scoop to scoop balls out of the other melon half. Place the balls in a bowl.
5. Place a number on the skewer. Slip the corresponding number of melon balls on the skewer.
6. Continue counting melon balls and placing them on the skewers with their corresponding numeral.
7. Place the Number Skewers on a plate and serve as a fruit snack. Serve with a dip of yogurt mixed with honey, if desired.

Serves 2 or more

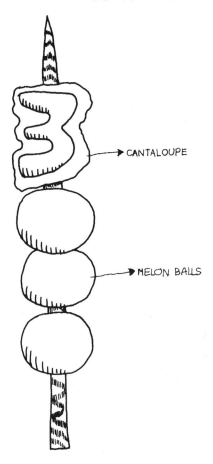
CANTALOUPE

MELON BALLS

easiest   about 30 minutes   bake   vegetable

Sweet Potato Writers

Serves 1 or more, depending on the amount of leftover potatoes

Ingredients

leftover mashed sweet potatoes

Utensils

spoon
pastry bag (use a plastic sandwich bag with a corner cut off for a substitute)
microwave-safe serving plate or cookie sheet

Process

1. Spoon the mashed sweet potatoes into a pastry bag.
2. Squeeze the potatoes onto the serving plate, spelling out words.
3. Place the potatoes in the microwave and warm for 3 to 4 minutes (or warm in the oven on a cookie sheet that has been sprayed with nonstick cooking spray).
4. Serve on a plate as part of a dinner, such as with baked chicken or fish, salad and bread.

Veggie Bundles

vegetable   bake   about 45 minutes   easy

Ingredients

2 to 3 carrots   10 scallions

10 asparagus spears   10 green beans

bacon strips, precooked but not crispy

Utensils

vegetable peeler   4 paper plates   knife and cutting board

baking sheet   saucepans   oven mitt

spatula   oven preheated to 350°F

Process

1. Scrape the carrots with the vegetable peeler until they are clean. Trim both ends off of each carrot.
2. Cut the carrots into long strips (this can be difficult, so any strips are fine). Fill a saucepan nearly full with water and add the carrot strips.
3. Place the pan of carrots on the stove and bring to a boil for 2 minutes. Remove the carrots from the heat. Drain water. Cool.
4. Put carrot strips on a paper plate.
5. Cook the green beans, asparagus and scallions, repeating the above procedure followed for cooking the carrots. Before cooking green beans trim both tips, and trim root end of asparagus. Use separate saucepans for each vegetable (or rinse saucepan before cooking each vegetable).
6. Place each variety of cooled and drained vegetable on a separate paper plate.
7. Gather one of each of the vegetables and make a bundle.
8. Wrap a bacon strip around the bundle and tie the ends in a knot. Place the bundles on the baking sheet.
9. Place the baking sheet in the oven and bake for 3 to 4 minutes, just until the bundles are thoroughly heated. Wear an oven mitt and remove the bundles from the oven. Transfer the Veggie Bundles with a spatula onto each individual plate. Add the other foods to complete the meal and serve.

▲ Counting vegetables in the bundles is part of the fun.

Serves 1 bundle per person

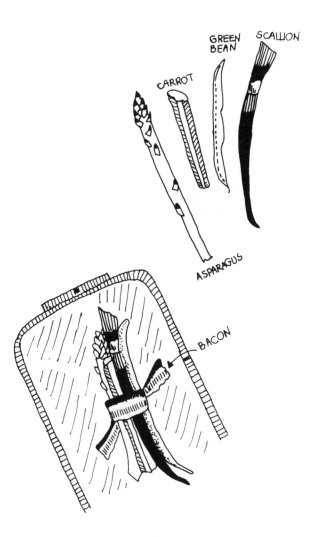

easiest   about 30 minutes   breakfast

Abacus Waffles

Serves 1 to 2 waffles per person

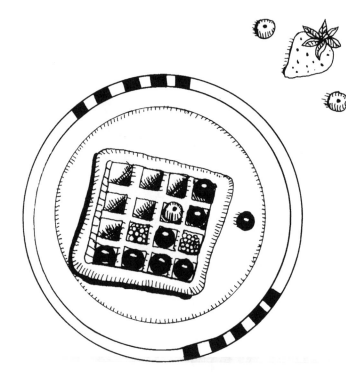

Ingredients

fresh assorted berries, such as
   blueberries, raspberries, blackberries, strawberries
box frozen waffles
blueberry or other flavored syrup

Utensils

serving bowls
spoon

Process

1. Place the blueberries or other fresh berries in a serving bowl. Set aside.
2. Heat the frozen waffles in the toaster according to package directions. Remove waffles carefully and place them on a plate.
3. Look at the rows of holes or compartments in the waffles.
4. Place one berry in the first square in the first row.
5. Place 2 berries in the first two squares of the second row. (Create your own pattern by using different types of berries or alternating the berries and colors.)
6. Place 3 berries in the first three squares of the third row. Continue adding the blueberries according to the numbers until all the rows have some berries. Make as many waffles per person as desired.
7. Each person pours syrup on his waffle before eating, if desired.
▲ Berry designs can be made in any pattern in the waffle holes.

Cowpoke Cakes

breakfast   about 30 minutes   easier

Ingredients

Serves 1 or more

frozen pancake mix or homemade mix
4 tablespoons vegetable oil
butter, warm syrup or jam
strawberry and parsley sprig, optional

Utensils

electric skillet, griddle or large frying pan
clean squeeze bottle
large spoon
¼ cup measuring cup
spatula

Process

1. Thaw the frozen pancake batter.
2. Pour the oil into the electric skillet.
3. Turn the electric skillet on medium heat.
4. Spoon the pancake batter into the squeeze bottle. (This can be a very messy job.)
5. Squeeze the batter in the shape of a letter into the skillet.
6. When the letter has lightly browned on the bottom side, pour about ¼ cup of
   batter over the top of it. Cook the design cake until bubbles show and edges are dry.
7. Turn the cowpoke cake over to cook the other side.
8. Carefully remove the cowpoke cake from the skillet with the spatula.
9. Place the cowpoke cake on the serving plate with the design side showing. If desired,
   decorate the top of the cake with a strawberry and parsley. Serve with butter, warm syrup
   or jam.
▲ Spell a word, name or message with pancakes. Create one letter for each pancake and then
   spread the cakes out on a plate or platter to be read and enjoyed.

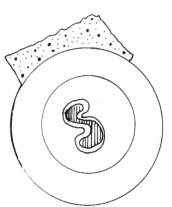

MAKE EACH
LETTER
SEPARATELY

easiest

10 to 15 minutes

bake

sandwich

AB C-heese Broil

Serves 1 per person

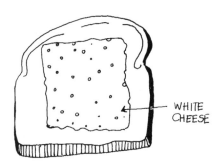

WHITE CHEESE

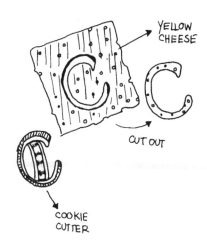

YELLOW CHEESE

CUT OUT

COOKIE CUTTER

Ingredients

1 package white cheese slices
1 package yellow cheese slices
1 slice of bread for each person

Utensils

letter cookie cutters or sharp knife
baking sheet
oven mitt

Process

1. Select a word (or letter) to place on the sandwich.
2. Place one slice of white cheese on the bread.
3. Place the yellow cheese on the work surface.
4. Choose the letters of the cookie cutters for the word selected.
5. Press the cookie cutters in the yellow cheese or cut out letters with a sharp knife.
6. Peel the letters out of the cheese. Spell the word by placing the letters on the white cheese that is on the bread.
7. Place the slice of bread on the baking sheet.
8. Turn the oven on broil. Place the baking sheet under the broiler for a few minutes until the cheese melts. Watch carefully so the cheese does not burn. Wear an oven mitt and remove the baking sheet from the oven.
9. Place the cheese sandwich on a plate to serve.

Cooking Art

Sentence Sandwiches

Ingredients

fruit jelly
sliced bread
alphabet cereal

Utensils

plates
spreading knife

Process

1. Place a slice of bread on each plate.
2. Spread the fruit jelly on each slice of bread.
3. Spread a handful of the cereal on a plate.
4. Select the appropriate letters to form initials, words and simple sentences.
5. Place the letters on the bread slices, forming sentences and maybe even a secret message!

Allow 1 slice of bread per person

Counting Cookies

Serves 5 to 10

COOKIE DOUGH

WALNUT SIZE

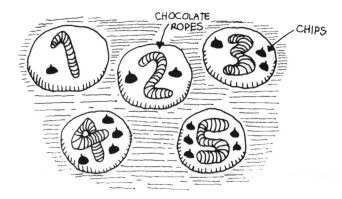

CHOCOLATE ROPES

CHIPS

Ingredients

nonstick cooking spray
refrigerated sugar cookie dough
refrigerated chocolate cookie dough
raisins, currants or chocolate chips, optional

Utensils

oven preheated to 350°F
baking sheet

Process

1. Spray a light coating of cooking spray on the baking sheet.
2. Pinch off about a walnut-size ball of dough from the roll of refrigerated sugar cookie dough. Press the ball onto the baking sheet so it is a flattened circle. Continue making the cookies using the above steps until all of the dough is used.
3. Pinch off about a walnut-size ball of dough from the roll of refrigerated chocolate cookie dough. Roll the dough into a rope, and continue making ropes until all of the dough is used.
4. Arrange a rolled chocolate rope on each of the plain sugar cookie circles, forming a numeral shape on each one.
5. Lightly pat each chocolate numeral into place on the plain sugar cookie circle.
6. If desired, add the corresponding number of raisins or chocolate chips on the cookies. For instance, add one raisin or chocolate chip for the numeral one, three raisins or chocolate chips for the numeral three, and so on.
7. Place the baking sheet in the oven and bake according to the package directions, usually about 8 minutes. Wear an oven mitt and remove the baking sheet from the oven. Let the cookies cool briefly.
8. Remove the cookies with a spatula to a serving tray or platter. Count the delicious cookies as they disappear!

Chapter 5

Building & Construction

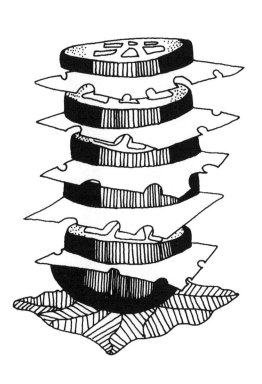

Cuppacup Layered Salad

Serves 2 to 6

Ingredients

1 cup each
broccoli florets
shredded lettuce
cooked green peas

grated carrot
cauliflower florets
creamy herb salad dressing

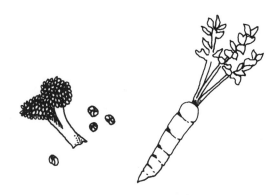

Utensils

knife and cutting board
5 small bowls
clear plastic or glass salad bowl, large enough to hold five cups of vegetables

Process

1. Prepare the vegetables and separate them into small bowls.
2. Put one layer of a vegetable in the bottom of the clear salad bowl.
3. Select a different color vegetable and place it on top of the first layer.
4. Select a different color vegetable and place on top of the first two layers.
5. Continue layering the salad until all of the vegetables are used.
6. Slowly pour the salad dressing over the top of the salad like icing.
7. Serve the layered salad with a large serving spoon as part of a meal or for a complete light lunch.

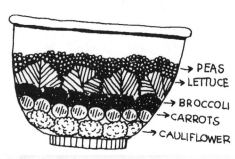

→ PEAS
→ LETTUCE
→ BROCCOLI
→ CARROTS
→ CAULIFLOWER

Melon Tower

fruit

about 30 minutes

easiest

Ingredients

Serves 8 to 10

cantaloupe or honeydew melon
parsley
choice of fruits, such as
    strawberries, cherries, kiwi fruit, canned pineapple

Utensils

knife and cutting board
spoon
toothpicks

Process

1. Cut the melon in half. Scrape the seeds out of the melon.
2. Cut the skin off the melon.
3. Cut the melon into slices.
4. Make a layer of melon slices by placing them around the outer edge of the plate. Leave about ½ inch of space between the slices. See the illustration.
5. Add the next layer of melon slices, overlapping the ends of the melon sections of the first layer. See the illustration. This should resemble commonly seen brick patterns in buildings. Continue building the tower until it is 5 or 6 levels high.
6. Look at the outside of the structure. Decide where to add decorative features.
7. Slice, cube or cut the other fruits in any way. Berries can be left whole.
8. Stick a toothpick through a piece of fruit. Stick the toothpick with the piece of fruit on it to the melon tower to decorate it. Continue with this step until the melon is decorated as desired.
9. Garnish with parsley at the base of the melon tower and place the plate on a table with a serving fork or toothpicks.

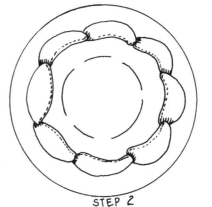
STEP 2

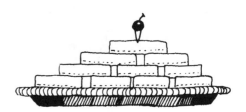

easiest   10 to 15 minutes   vegetable

Tomato Tower

One tomato tower serves 2 to 4 people

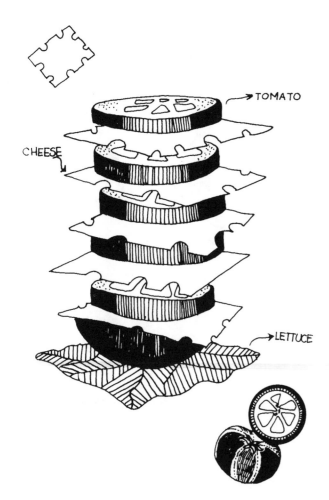

TOMATO

CHEESE

LETTUCE

Ingredients

2 firm, large tomatoes
sliced cheese
shredded lettuce
optional foods sliced in circles, such as
  slice of green pepper, circle slice of bread,
  circle of flour tortilla
optional spreading cheeses or dips, such as
  cream cheese, can of squirt cheese, thick vegetable dip

→ TOP

→ BOTTOM

Utensils

knife
paper towels

Process

1. Slice the tomatoes horizontally into at least 4 slices. Save the top and bottom of one tomato. See the illustration.
2. Place each tomato slice on a paper towel for 5 minutes to drain the moisture.
3. Find the bottom part of the tomato and place it on the plate.
4. Place one slice of cheese on the sliced side of the bottom tomato.
5. Select a tomato slice and place it on top of the cheese.
▲ Add layers of the optional foods too, if desired.
6. Place another cheese slice on top of this tomato slice.
7. Place another tomato slice on top of the cheese.
8. Continue building the tomato tower until all of the tomato slices are used.
9. Spread the lettuce around the bottom of the tomato and serve. The tower can be eaten with a knife and fork, or pulled apart and eaten with fingers.

Build-It Party Sandwich

Ingredients

Serves 20

¼ cup margarine
1 tablespoon lemon juice
5 thin slices of natural white bread
20 thin tomato slices

⅛ teaspoon salt
3 ounces cream cheese
10 thin slices whole grain bread
20 thin cucumber slices

Utensils

medium mixing bowl and spoon
knife and cutting board
toothpicks
teaspoon

small round biscuit cutter or cookie cutter
spreading knife
wax paper

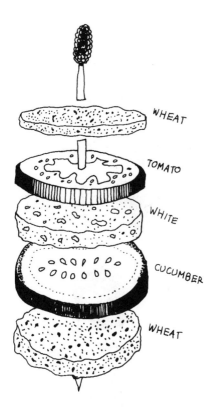

Process

1. Mix together the margarine, lemon juice, salt and cream cheese in a bowl. Set aside.
2. With the small round cookie cutter, cut four circles from each white bread slice (20 total), and four circles from each whole wheat slice (40 total).
3. Using the same cutter, cut one circle from each tomato and cucumber slice. Use the scraps of vegetables for other salad recipes. Use the bread scraps to feed the birds, make croutons or to make bread stuffing.
4. Spread ½ teaspoon cream cheese mixture on both sides of each white bread circle and set aside on wax paper. Spread cheese mixture on one side of each wheat circle.
5. To assemble the small stack sandwich, follow this pattern:
   ✔ wheat bread
   ✔ tomato
   ✔ white bread
   ✔ cucumber
   ✔ wheat bread
6. Poke each stack with a toothpick to secure, and serve as party or lunch sandwiches.

easiest   about 30 minutes   sandwich

Apple High-Rise Sandwich

Serves 2 to 4

Ingredients

2 to 4 medium apples
sliced cheeses
sliced luncheon meats
parsley

Utensils

knife and cutting board
apple corer
table knife

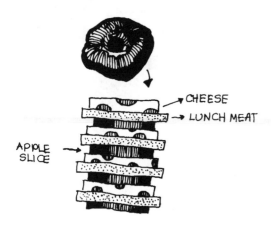

Process

1. Cut a thin slice from the tops and bottoms of each apple with a knife. Set aside.
2. Core the remaining portions of the apples.
3. Cut the apples into 8 horizontal slices, about $1/3$-inch thick. See illustration.
4. Stack the cheese and cut it into 4 equal pieces.
5. Stack the luncheon meats and cut into 4 equal pieces.
6. Place the bottom of each apple on the plate.
7. Create a pattern by stacking the luncheon meat, cheese and apple slices, or invent other patterns of layers.
8. Set the stem slices on top of the stacks.
9. Arrange the parsley around the bottom of the apples to garnish.

Cooking Art

Little Log Buildings

Ingredients

Serves 2 to 4

⅓ cup peanut butter
3 tablespoons honey
½ cup crushed corn flakes
½ cup quick oatmeal
¼ cup dry milk
chocolate sprinkles

Utensils

measuring cups and spoons
mixing bowl
wooden spoon
baking sheet

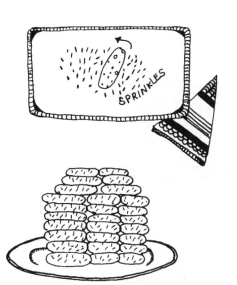

Process

1. Place the peanut butter and honey in a mixing bowl and mix well with the wooden spoon.
2. Add the corn flakes, oatmeal and milk to the peanut butter mixture and mix well.
3. Pinch off a small amount of the dough mixture.
4. Roll the small amount of dough into 2-inch-long by ½-inch-wide logs.
5. Place the sprinkles on the baking sheet.
6. Roll the logs in sprinkles.
7. Stack the logs on a plate on top of one another in a building formation.
8. Serve the building as a yummy dessert.

Dipped Bricks

Serves 3 to 8

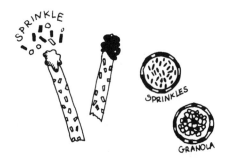

Ingredients

1 cup semisweet-chocolate chips
bar (3 ounces) white chocolate, broken into small pieces
pretzel rods
suggested decorations, such as
    sprinkles, nuts, coconut, granola

Utensils

2 small microwave-safe bowls or saucepans
2 wooden spoons
wire cooling rack
wax paper
fruits, candies, raisins, candles, toothpicks, small clean toys, optional
ice cream, optional
cookie cutters, optional

Process

1. Place the chocolate chips in a small microwave-safe bowl or saucepan.
2. Microwave the chocolate chips on medium for 2 minutes, then stir. The chocolate can also be melted in a saucepan.
3. Take the chocolate out of the microwave (or off the stove) and let stand about 1 minute, then stir again until smooth.
4. Place the white chocolate in another bowl. Microwave the white chocolate on medium for 2 minutes, then stir. The white chocolate can also be melted in a saucepan.
5. Let stand about 1 minute, then stir again until smooth.
6. Decorate each pretzel rod by dipping one end of each pretzel into either of the melted chocolates. (Or dip a pretzel into one chocolate, let it set briefly, then drizzle the other chocolate with a spoon over the first.)
7. Before the chocolate dries, sprinkle decorations onto dipped ends of pretzels.
8. Place the pretzels on a wire rack until chocolate is dry.
9. Stack the pretzel bricks on a serving platter, one on top of another as if constructing a building, before serving.

Cubed Cake Sculpture

Serves many

Ingredients

prebaked white or yellow cake without icing
frosting, canned or favorite recipe
food coloring

Utensils

muffin tins	knife and cutting board
spoons	spreading knives

wax paper and baking sheet or piece of cardboard
pastry bag (use a plastic sandwich bag with a corner cut off for a substitute)

Process

1. Cover the baking sheet or piece of cardboard with wax paper. This will be the area where the sculpture will be built. Set aside.

2. Cut the cake into cubes of different sizes. Set aside.

3. Place white frosting in different sections of muffin tins. Put a few drops of food coloring in each muffin tin section and mix well. Use a different spoon for each color when mixing the food colorings.

▲ Chocolate frosting cannot be colored, but it can be used as a brown color in this sculpture.

4. Spread a little frosting on the wax paper so the base of the sculpture will not fall over.

5. Spread some frosting on a piece of cake and stick it to the frosted wax paper. Frost more cubes and build a sculpture adding cake cubes with different colors of frosting. The frosting acts like glue.

6. When the sculpture is complete, add more frosting as desired. Squeeze frosting on the sculpture to add other designs and features. Add some green frosting around the base of the sculpture for grass and some other features to make it look like a building.

▲ If desired, decorate the cubed cake with fruits, candies, raisins, candles, toothpicks or small clean toys. Serve the cake with little scoops of different kinds of ice cream or sherbet that have been prescooped, placed in a shallow bowl and frozen. Each person can add small scoops of colorful ice cream or sherbet to his own sculpture. Cakes can be cut into any variety of shapes using cookie cutters or a knife, such as a bunny, tree, heart, clown, ball or geometric shape.

Graham Cracker Cottage

Serves 2 to 6

Ingredients

For the icing

3 egg whites	1 box confectioners' sugar
1 teaspoon vanilla	½ teaspoon cream of tartar

For the cottage construction

box of graham crackers

variety of decorations, such as

lifesavers	Necco wafers	swirled cinnamon mints
M&Ms	coconut shavings	gummie bears
nuts	chocolate chips	sprinkles
candy canes	pretzel sticks	licorice sticks
brown sugar	sugar cubes	animal crackers
jelly beans	cookies	chocolate bar squares
mini-gingerbread		

Utensils

heavy piece of cardboard	aluminum foil
mixing bowl	electric mixer
plastic wrap	pastry bag with tips (or plastic bags)
spreading knife or spatula	bowls for frosting

Process

1. Prepare the base for the cottage by covering the heavy cardboard with aluminum foil. Set aside.
2. Whip the egg whites with an electric mixer until fluffy. Add the cream of tartar and vanilla. Stir in 1 box of confectioners' sugar a little at a time.
3. Spoon this egg white icing glue into the pastry bag. If there is any icing left, cover the bowl with plastic wrap and set aside for another recipe.
▲ Instead of a pastry bag, use a sandwich bag with a bit of one corner cut off.
4. Using a spreading knife or spatula, spread about ¼ inch of frosting on the surface of the foil-covered cardboard.

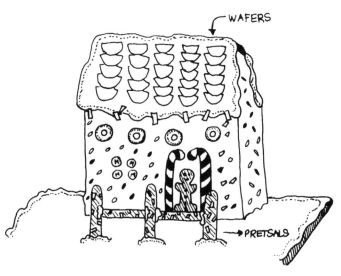

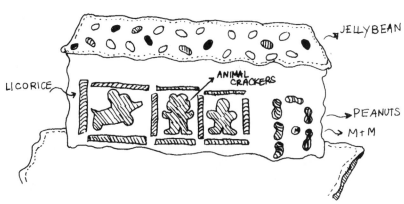

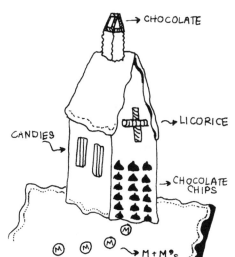

5. Gently press one large graham cracker face down into the frosting as the base of the cottage. Let sit for several minutes to harden.

6. Add the walls of the cottage by gluing more graham cracker pieces into place with egg white icing. Let harden. Then, add a graham cracker roof in the same way. Harden.

7. Decorate the cottage by adding more frosting from the pastry tube or with the spreading knife. Stick candies and other decorations into the frosting on the roof, walls, yard and so on. Some suggestions are pretzel sticks for fences and railings, Necco wafers for shingles on the roof, lifesavers for windows and grated coconut for icicles.

▲ The cottage may be any type of building such as a church, school, playhouse, train station or store.

8. For additional decoration, cover the cardboard base with more frosting and decorate the yard with a sidewalk, fences, duck pond and so on.

▲ Create an entire village by combining creations in a group like a village or town. A graham cracker cottage makes a delightful centerpiece. When ready to eat, simply break and pull pieces off the construction as desired. Cooking artists may wish to take a picture of the graham cracker cottage before taking it apart.

Toastie Arctic Igloo

Serves 12

SCOOP

CUPCAKE

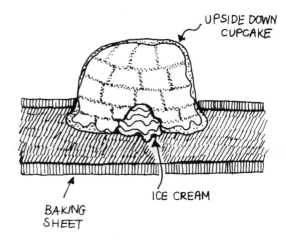

UPSIDE DOWN CUPCAKE

ICE CREAM

BAKING SHEET

Ingredients

12 prebaked cupcakes, any flavor
1 quart ice cream, any flavor
12 egg whites
1 cup sugar

Utensils

spoons	bowl
spreading knives	electric mixer
oven mitts	baking sheet

Process

1. With a regular spoon, scoop out the center of each cupcake. Eat the centers for fun, give to the birds or save for another recipe.
2. Next, fill the centers of each cupcake with ice cream, any flavor. The hard part is to freeze them overnight until solid.
3. The next day, when almost time to enjoy this dessert, make the topping for the arctic cupcake igloo. Put the egg whites in a bowl. Whip all the whites with an electric mixer until stiff and fluffy. Then, continue to whip the whites and add the sugar a little at a time until somewhat thicker and creamier.
4. Place one of the frozen cupcakes on the baking sheet. Spread egg whites on the cupcake, creating a small, white, snowy igloo. Score lines in the whites with the spreading knife to create the blocks of snow. Make as many igloos as desired.
▲ Make all 12 igloo cupcakes at once, or make a few at a time while the others stay cold in the freezer.
5. Slide the igloos into the oven under the broiler for 3 to 5 minutes, or until the igloos are lightly browned on top. Wear oven mitts and remove the igloos from the oven.
6. Serve this dessert quickly before it melts.

Chapter 6

Transportation & Travel

easy about 45 minutes salad

Airplane Cucumbers

Serves 2 — one-half of a cucumber (1 airplane) each

Ingredients

1 medium cucumber
1 small red bell pepper
lettuce shredded
slices of carrot for wings and tail parts
foods to add to the airplane, if desired, such as

grated carrot	chopped tomato	chopped celery	sliced mushrooms
peas	apple bits	grapes	tofu cubes
sesame seeds	almonds	pine nuts	peanuts
parsley	kidney beans	corn	

cheddar, Parmesan, Romano or feta cheese

dark green lettuce leaves to line the plate
one-half of a small onion
favorite salad dressing (about 4 tablespoons)

Utensils

knife and cutting board
grapefruit spoon, regular spoon or melon ball scoop
small bowl
kitchen towel
fork

Process

1. Slice the cucumber in half lengthwise with a knife. Using the grapefruit spoon, regular spoon or melon ball scoop, hollow out a hole in the center of each cucumber half where the seeds are found. The hole should be 1/8 inch or so from the edge of the cucumber all the way around it. The cucumber will resemble a hollowed out airplane fuselage.
2. Place a dark green lettuce leaf on each plate to resemble the earth below the flying airplane. Place the cucumber halves on the lettuce earth, one for each airplane.
3. Next cut off the top of the red bell pepper and then cut it in half. Scoop out the seeds and soft pulp from the sides. Dice the pepper and place the pieces in a bowl. Dice the half onion and add to the bowl of diced red pepper.

Cooking Art

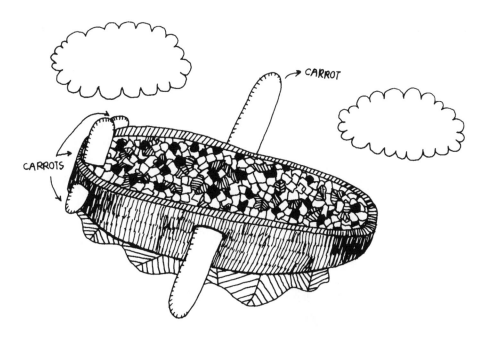

4. Place the lettuce in the bowl with the onion and red pepper. Other food choices may be added to the salad mixture at this time, but are not required.

5. Combine the ingredients in the bowl with a fork to make the salad stuffing for the cucumber airplanes. Mix in salad dressing to moisten the ingredients.

6. Stuff the holes in the cucumber airplanes with the salad ingredients for cargo.

7. To create the wings and tail parts, place a carrot on the cutting board and, holding with one hand, slice through it on a diagonal with a knife. Slice 2 long diagonal slices for the wings and three smaller ones for the tail pieces. See illustrations.

8. Cut a slit on each side of the airplane fuselage for the wings and cut three small slits in the tail. Insert the carrot slices to resemble two wings and a three-piece tail.

9. Serve and enjoy as a salad that flies high in taste and nutrition.

Banana Boats

Serves 1 person per banana

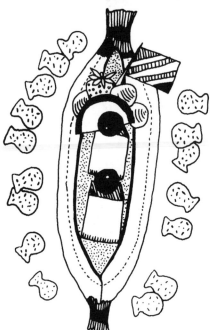

Ingredients

bananas
lemon juice in a small cup, at least 2 tablespoons
any choices of favorite fruits, such as

watermelon	cantaloupe	strawberries
pineapple	berries	apple slices

fish crackers

Utensils

knife and cutting board
spoon
pastry brush
sandwich pick or toothpick with paper sail, optional

Process

1. Place the unpeeled banana on the cutting board so it curves upright like a boat.
2. Find the natural ridges of the banana.
3. Cut a long slice down one side on the inside curve of the banana, around the end and up the other side of the banana with a knife (but not all the way through the banana). This cut forms a large hole in the curved side of the banana. See illustration.
4. Peel the cut-out section only, not the whole banana.
5. Scoop out some of the banana inside.
6. Dip the pastry brush into the lemon juice and paint the inside of the banana with lemon juice to prevent it from turning brown.
7. Cut favorite fruits into designs, sections and shapes. Arrange the fruits inside the banana boats like people and cargo riding inside.
8. Add a sandwich pick with a paper sail, if desired.
9. Sprinkle fish crackers around the banana boat.
▲ Sail away to snack time!

Cantaloupe Canoes

fruit

10 to 15 minutes

easier

Ingredients

Serves 2 to 4

1 firm, ripe cantaloupe
selection of fresh fruits, such as

raspberries	blueberries	grapes
strawberries	pineapple chunks	melon balls
cherries	banana slices	

yogurt, any flavor
fresh lettuce leaves

Utensils

knife and cutting board
spoon
small cookie cutters, any shapes

Process

1. Cut the cantaloupe in half with a knife. Cut the halves in half again so they are the shapes of wedges or canoes. Scoop the seeds from the four cantaloupe canoes with a spoon. Trim the skin from all four canoes.
2. Press a small cookie cutter into the side of the cantaloupe canoes to cut away design holes. See the illustration. Make design holes with cookie cutters in all four canoes.
3. Place the canoes on a plate lined with fresh lettuce leaves.
4. Decorate around the canoes with other fruit, and fill the holes in the wedges with assorted berries or grapes.
5. Drizzle yogurt over the tops of the cantaloupe canoes with a spoon.
6. Put the cantaloupe canoes on a plate and arrange lettuce leaves around them.
7. Decorate with more fruits.

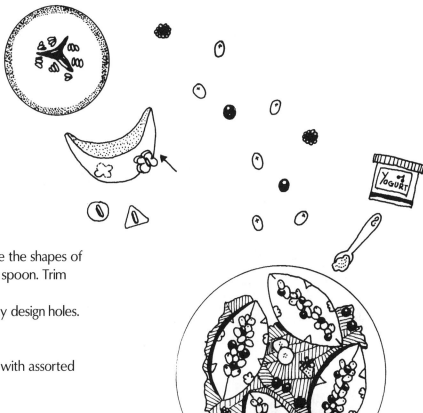

Baked Potato Submarine

One potato serves 2 people

Ingredients

baking potatoes, one-half per person
vegetable oil
3 tablespoons soft butter
milk
salt and pepper, optional
vegetables for decoration, such as

mushroom stems	parsley leaves	broccoli florets
red pepper sticks	cherry tomatoes	green beans

lettuce

Utensils

oven preheated to 400°F	vegetable scrub brush
baking sheet	oven mitt
fork	spoon
knife	bowl
potato masher, optional	

Process

1. Scrub each potato under running water with the vegetable brush. Then, pour a little vegetable oil into your hand and rub each potato with oil.
2. Place potatoes on a baking sheet and prick the skins with a fork. Bake the potatoes in the oven for 1½ hours or until a knife inserts easily through the center of the potato.
3. Wear an oven mitt and remove the potatoes from the oven. Let cool for 15 minutes. Cut the potatoes in half lengthwise, from end to end.
4. Scoop out the soft white center from each potato half with a spoon and put this scooped out pulp in a bowl. Try not to break the potato skins when scooping because it will be needed to form the boat shape.

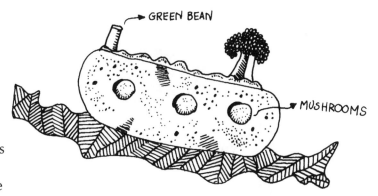

GREEN BEAN

MUSHROOMS

5. Add softened butter to the potato pulp in the bowl and mash together with a fork or a potato masher. Add a little milk and mix. (A few tablespoons of milk per potato half works well.) Salt and pepper can be added now, if desired.

6. Mound the mashed potato mixture back into the potato skin submarine. Pat and press the potato mixture into the submarine with the back of a spoon or by hand so that it is level with the top edge of the skin.

7. Put the stuffed-potato submarines in the oven for 15 minutes to warm. Wear an oven mitt and remove the potato submarines from the oven. Carefully remove each potato submarine from the baking sheet and place it on a serving dish.

8. Decorate each potato submarine with the remaining ingredients. Consider making features and parts seen on any boat, or only submarine features, such as

sails	oars	periscope
tugboat funnels	flags	smoke stack
portholes	ropes and lines	

9. Spread lettuce on the plate to resemble the green, rolling waves, if desired, and serve while still warm.

Zucchini Freight Train

Serves 2 or more

ROUND OFF

HOLLOW OUT

CARROT STICKS

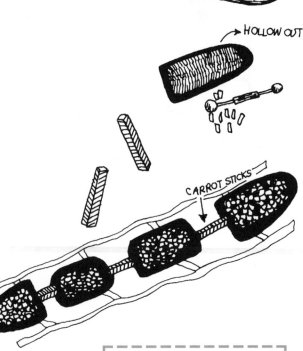

Serve for lunch or dinner.
Here comes the Zucchini
Freight Train on Track No. 9!

Ingredients

large zucchini for the train
1 teaspoon butter, optional
1 package mixed frozen vegetables for freight
cooked and cooled extra long spaghetti noodles for the track

carrot sticks to join the train cars
salt and pepper, optional

Utensils

serving tray covered with wax paper
grapefruit spoon or melon ball scoop

knife and cutting board
small bowl

Process

1. Place two long strings of spaghetti noodles on the wax paper-covered serving tray. Then, cut three spaghetti noodles into 3-inch pieces. Place the 3-inch pieces of spaghetti noodles across the long spaghetti noodles to create a train track.

2. Slice the zucchini in half lengthwise with a knife. Cut the zucchini halves into 3- or 4-inch sections. Carve the ends of the zucchini pieces somewhat rounded at each end to resemble train cars.

3. Using a grapefruit spoon or a melon ball scoop, hollow out a hole in the center of each zucchini section. The hole should be about 1/8 inch from the edge of the zucchini all the way around it. Save the scrapings for a salad or pizza recipe.

4. Poke a hole in the ends of each zucchini section with the point of a knife. However, for two sections — the engine and caboose — poke only one hole.

5. Stick the carrot sticks through the holes of the zucchini to attach the sections of the train cars together. Place the engine and the caboose (with only one hole each) at the front and back of the train. Join with carrot sticks.

6. When the train cars are joined, arrange the zucchini train on the train tracks. It may come apart but can be easily reassembled.

7. Next, put some of the mixed vegetables in the small bowl. Place the small bowl of vegetables in the microwave (or in a saucepan) and cook on medium until warmed through. Remove the cooked vegetables and mix in a little butter and salt and pepper, if desired. Spoon the mixed vegetables into the open holes in the zucchini train.

Rollin' Along Hamwich

sandwich

about 45 minutes

easier

Ingredients

Serves 2

½ small package cream cheese
1 tablespoon mayonnaise
2 square slices of bread

1 teaspoon mustard, and a little extra
2 slices of packaged ham slices, plus more
1 slice of cheese

Utensils

mixing bowl and spoon
toothpicks
paper plate

spreading knife
knife and cutting board
permanent markers

Process

1. Make a spread by stirring together the following ingredients: cream cheese, mayonnaise and a little mustard. Set aside.
2. Put the ham slices on the work surface. Spread the cream cheese mixture evenly on one side of each ham slice.
3. Roll up each ham slice in jelly roll fashion. Secure the roll with a toothpick to hold. Chill the ham rolls in the refrigerator for 1 hour. Then, remove.
4. Slice each ham roll into 1-inch pieces, making four small rolls. These will be the wheels for the ham and cheese sandwich.
5. To make the sandwich, place one slice of bread on the work surface. Spread with 1 teaspoon or more of mustard. Place a slice of cheese on the bread and a slice of ham on the cheese. Top the sandwich with another slice of bread.
6. Cut the sandwich in half to form two rectangles. Crusts may be removed or left on.
7. Draw a simple road with a permanent marker on a paper plate. Line a lunch plate with the paper plate. Place each sandwich half on one of the roads.
8. Position the ham roll wheels underneath and at the edge of each sandwich rectangle corner to create Hamwich cars.
▲ Serve the cars for a moving, rolling lunch or snack.

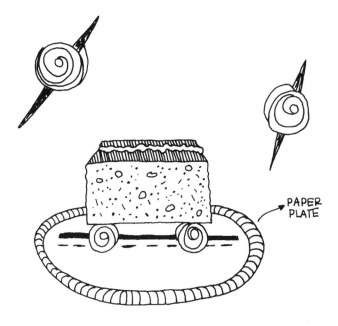

PAPER PLATE

Chili Boats

Serves 4

SCOOP OUT

FRENCH ROLL

Ingredients

canned chili in a microwave-safe bowl
1 package of cheese slices
celery sticks

4 French rolls
carrot sticks

Utensils

bowl or saucepan
spoon
kitchen scissors

small microwave-safe bowls (one for each roll) or baking sheet
knife and cutting board
oven mitts

Process

1. Warm the chili in a bowl in the microwave on medium for 4 minutes. The chili can also be warmed in a saucepan.
2. Cut the French rolls then or scoop out a circle of bread from the top of the roll to form a cavity or bowl in the roll. Try not to make a hole that goes all the way through the roll or the boat will leak.
3. Place each roll in a small microwave-safe bowl or on a baking sheet. Scoop the warm chili into the empty cavity in each roll.
4. Next, cut the cheese into shapes or patterns with the knife or kitchen scissors. Place the shapes on the tops of each chili boat in a design or pattern.
5. Place the chili boats in the microwave and warm on medium until the chili is warmed through and the cheese is slightly melted, about 4 minutes. Check after 2 minutes. The chili boats can also be warmed in the oven. Wear an oven mitt and remove the chili boats from the microwave (or oven).
6. Place the chili boats on a serving plate. Arrange carrot sticks and celery sticks on the plate around the bowl to resemble oars. If desired, dip the celery and carrots into the chili while eating.
7. Serve with extra napkins and a fork.

Fishing Boats

Ingredients

Serves 4 or more

½ cup frozen vegetables, such as
    peas, corn, carrots or beans
a little water
8 frozen fish patties or sticks
mashed potatoes, instant or left-over, warmed and soft
carrot sticks, optional

Utensils

saucepan	oven mitts	pastry bag with large star tip
2 baking sheets	spatula	spoon
colander or strainer		

sandwich picks or toothpicks and paper triangle for a sail
oven preheated to 375°F or according to package directions

POTATO

Process

1. Place the frozen vegetables in a saucepan with a little water. Cook over medium heat until vegetables are warmed through. Drain and set aside.
2. Bake the fish patties in the oven on a baking sheet according to package directions. Keep them warm while preparing the potatoes.
3. Spoon the warm, soft mashed potatoes into a pastry bag fitted with a large star tip. Squeeze the potatoes onto the baking sheet in 8 enclosed shapes, such as a circle, oval or other shape that has no open ends. These shapes will be the boats, so by leaving a dent or scoop in the middle of the potato shape, more decorating possibilities will be available. Make them slightly smaller than the fish. See illustration.
4. Place the potato boats in the oven under the broiler until boats turn golden. This happens quickly so watch carefully. Wear an oven mitt and remove the potato boats from the broiler. Set aside while preparing the fish.
5. Move the fish from the pan to the serving plates with a spatula.
6. Remove the potatoes from the baking sheet with the spatula and place them on top of the fish. Decorate the inside of the potatoes with the remaining vegetables and serve immediately. Add a sandwich pick with a paper sail to complete the fishing boat design, if desired, or add carrot sticks for oars.

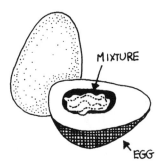
Sailboat Eggs

Allow 1 egg per sailor

Ingredients

hard-boiled eggs
½ teaspoon mustard
carrot sticks
chopped pimentos

1 teaspoon mayonnaise
1 cup diced green peppers
celery sticks
lettuce leaves

Utensils

knife and cutting board
bowl
fork
toothpicks for mast
scissors
paper for sails
tape

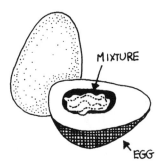

MIXTURE

EGG

Process

1. Peel the hard-boiled eggs. Discard shells or save for another art idea, such as eggshell mosaics.
2. Cut the eggs in half.
3. Remove the yolks and place them in a bowl.
4. Mash the yolks with 1 teaspoon mayonnaise and ½ teaspoon mustard.
5. Mound the mixture back into the egg white sections.
6. Decorate the egg sections with the celery sticks, carrot sticks and chopped pimentos.
7. Cut the paper into sails, attach to the toothpicks with tape and put into eggs.
8. Place the lettuce on a serving plate, then put the eggs on top of the lettuce.

Chapter 7

Flowers & Trees

Trees in Snow

Serves 1 — double or add to the recipe to serve more people

Ingredients
½ cup cottage cheese
broccoli florets, precooked, steamed lightly or raw uncooked
1 tablespoon Italian dressing

Utensils
measuring cup and spoon
small dish

Process
1. Spread the cottage cheese in a thick layer in the small dish.
2. Arrange the broccoli florets so they stand in the cottage cheese, resembling trees in the snow.
3. Drizzle a little Italian dressing over the broccoli florets to flavor the salad.
4. Serve the Trees in Snow with a fork as a healthy, tasty salad.

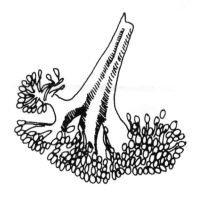

Poinsettia Salad

Ingredients

Serves 2 to 4

firm, ripe tomatoes
yellow food coloring or mustard
spinach leaves
¼ cup white ingredient, such as

| mayonnaise | cream cheese | sour cream |
| plain yogurt | salad dressing | |

Utensils

knife and cutting board
small cup
spoon
kitchen scissors

ADD YELLOW FOOD COLORING

MAYONNAISE OR CREAM CHEESE

Process

1. Slice the ripe tomatoes into wedges. Set aside
2. Add one drop of yellow food coloring or mustard to the white mayonnaise, cream cheese or other ingredient in a cup and mix.
3. Place a spoonful of the yellow dressing in the center of a small plate.
4. Arrange tomato wedges around the dressing to create the petals of a red poinsettia flower with a yellow center.
5. Tuck a few spinach leaves between the tomato wedges to add some green leaves. The leaves can be trimmed with kitchen scissors to be pointy like poinsettia leaves.
6. Serve as a holiday salad with a meal or for a light lunch.

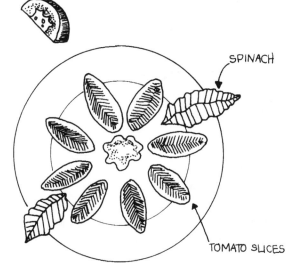

SPINACH

TOMATO SLICES

Potted Salad

Serves 2 to 4

Ingredients

favorite vegetable dip, such as
   Baba Ganouj
variety of raw, cut vegetables, such as

broccoli on stem	carrot sticks	green bell pepper slices
jicama slices	string beans	cauliflower
celery sticks	zucchini	cucumber sticks
sprouts	asparagus	summer squash
spinach leaves		

Utensils

coffee filter
small, clean terra cotta flower pot
knife and cutting board
spoons
natural dried weeds, grasses or raffia for decoration

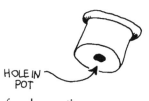 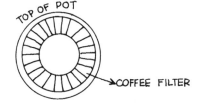

HOLE IN POT   TOP OF POT   COFFEE FILTER

Process

1. Place the coffee filter in the bottom of the flower pot to line the pot and cover the hole.
2. Spoon vegetable dip into the pot until about half full.
3. Arrange raw vegetables and vegetable sticks and slices in the pot to resemble a plant, bouquet or flower arrangement.
4. Add spinach leaves to make the arrangement look like it has leaves.
5. If desired, tie a natural bow made from long dried grasses, weeds or raffia around the pot to decorate.
6. Place the potted salad in the center of the table to serve as a healthy snack or an addition to a lunch to be shared by two to four people.

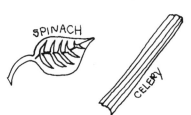  

SPINACH   CELERY   BROCCOLI   DRIED WEED

Baba Ganouj Dip

1 eggplant
one-half of a lemon
garlic powder
parsley
salt and pepper
Prepare Baba Ganouj ahead of time.
Preheat oven to 300°F. Pierce 1 eggplant with a fork and bake until the eggplant collapses (about 30 to 45 minutes). Let cool. Scoop out the eggplant with a spoon into a bowl and mash. Mix in garlic powder, juice of one-half lemon, 1 tablespoon chopped or dry parsley, ¼ teaspoon salt and a little pepper. Serve as a vegetable dip or spread for bread.

Cherry Tomato Blossoms

salad   about 30 minutes   easiest

Ingredients

Serves 5 to 10

½ pound cherry tomatoes
1 package dry salad dressing mix (any flavor)
fresh parsley sprigs
Romaine lettuce

¾ cup low-fat cream cheese
cucumber
scallions or green onions

Utensils

knife and cutting board
paper towels
pastry bag with small star tip

small spoon or demitasse spoon
small mixing bowl and spoon
fork

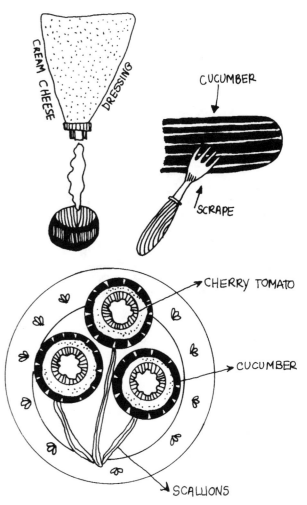

Process

1. Cut off cherry tomato tops with a knife. Discard the tomato tops or add to the compost pile. Carefully scoop out the insides of the cherry tomatoes with a small spoon.
2. Place the empty tomatoes upside down on a double thickness of paper towels to drain.
3. Mix the cream cheese and dry salad dressing in a small bowl. Then, put the cheese mixture in a pastry bag fitted with a small star tip.
4. Squeeze the cheese mixture into the tomato cavities. Fill all the tomatoes.
5. Scrape the prongs of a fork straight down the sides of a cucumber to etch lines in the skin. Slice the cucumbers into ¼ or 1/8 -inch slices.
6. Arrange 3 or 4 cucumber slices on a serving plate. Place one tomato on top of each cucumber slice to look like the blossom of a flower.
7. Place the parsley sprigs in the cheese-stuffed tomato to resemble leaves of a flower.
8. Arrange several green onions or scallions on the serving plate with bottom sections together and tops fanning out to resemble stems of flowers.
9. Set a tomato flower at the top of each scallion. Arrange the Romaine lettuce leaves near the scallions to look like leaves growing from a stem.

Stuffed Garden Salad

Serves 4

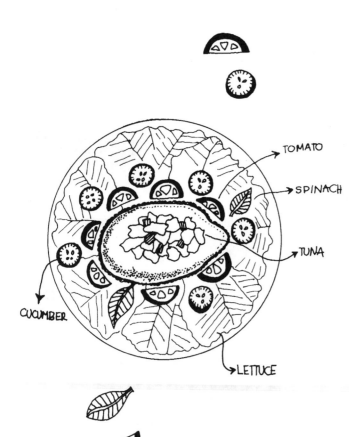

TOMATO

SPINACH

TUNA

CUCUMBER

LETTUCE

Ingredients

lettuce leaves
1 can tuna packed in water, drained
2 tablespoons lemon juice
2 tomatoes, sliced and peeled
selection of garden vegetables, such as
   cucumber circles
   celery leaves
   broccoli florets
vinegar and oil dressing, optional

2 avocados, halved (one-half per person)
½ cup diced celery
¼ cup light mayonnaise

carrot sticks
spinach leaves
cauliflower florets

Utensils

4 salad plates
knife and cutting board
small mixing bowl and spoon

Process

1. Cover the salad plates with lettuce leaves.
2. Slice the avocados in half and carefully remove the seeds from inside. Peel the thick skins from the four avocado halves.
3. Place each avocado half on the lettuce.
4. Mix the tuna, celery, lemon juice and mayonnaise in a bowl with a spoon.
5. Scoop the tuna salad into the center of each avocado half.
6. Arrange tomato slices around the avocado salad like flower petals.
7. Arrange other vegetables around the avocado to form imaginative garden blossoms.
8. Serve the garden salad as is or with a light vinegar and oil dressing for an outdoor patio summer lunch.

Biscuit Blossoms

bread

bake

about 30 minutes

easier

Ingredients

Serves 4 to 6

spinach leaves   refrigerator biscuits (or your favorite biscuit recipe)

choice of berries, such as

strawberries	blueberries
raspberries	blackberries

choice of fruits or nuts, such as

apple slices	pears	Mandarin orange sections
peaches	grapes	apricots
almonds		

Utensils

oven preheated to 375°F or according to package directions

paper towels	baking sheet	oven mitt
kitchen scissors	spatula	

Process

1. Wash the spinach leaves under running water and pat dry with paper towels. Set aside until later.
2. Open the package of biscuits and separate the biscuits from the roll. Snip tiny cuts around the edge of each biscuit with kitchen scissors to form flower petals. Other ways to form the biscuits into flower shapes include the following:
   ✔ cut biscuits in half and press them into flower shapes
   ✔ join several biscuits or pieces of biscuits together
   ✔ form the dough into shapes by hand
3. Place the biscuit blossoms about 2 inches apart on the baking sheet. Use a finger to press a dent in the biscuit where pieces of fruit will be placed. Place several pieces or a single piece of fruit in the indentation in each biscuit.
4. Bake the biscuits for about 10 minutes or until lightly golden brown. Wear an oven mitt and remove the biscuits from the oven. Cool a little.
5. Remove the Biscuit Blossoms from the baking sheet with a spatula and arrange them on the serving tray.
6. Place the spinach leaves around the blossoms to resemble leaves. Serve as a warm snack or as an addition to any meal.

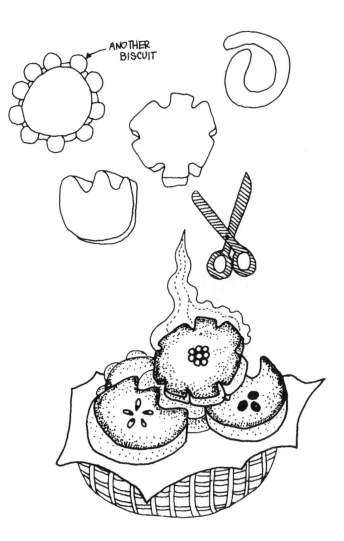
ANOTHER BISCUIT

Banana Tree

One banana tree per person — recipe can be "doubled or tripled easily" for more servings

Ingredients

lettuce leaf
pineapple ring
banana
sliced fruits, such as
   grapes
   cherries
   strawberries or other berries
cheese, cut in cubes

cut up pears
cut up peaches
apple slices or chunks

Utensils

knife and cutting board
toothpicks

Process

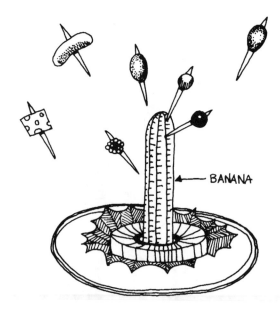

BANANA

1. Place a lettuce leaf on the salad plate.
2. Place a pineapple ring on the lettuce leaf.
3. Peel the banana and cut it in half.
4. Stand the cut end of the banana half in the center of the pineapple to resemble a tree trunk.
5. Place a toothpick through a selected piece of fruit.
6. Stick the other end of the toothpick into the top area of the banana. Each toothpick with a piece of fruit will represent a branch on the banana tree.
7. Fill the tree with as many fruit branches as desired. It may be necessary to hold the banana with one hand so it does not tip over when first beginning the work.
8. The banana trees can be served as fruit salad to be eaten with the fingers.

Pita Pocket Bouquet

sandwich   bake   about 45 minutes   easy

Ingredients

1 pita bread pocket
2 tablespoons grated provolone cheese
⅛ teaspoon dried basil
small pieces of fresh raw vegetables, such as

broccoli	carrot sticks
celery sticks	green bell peppers
scallions	cauliflower

¼ cup ricotta cheese
2 tablespoons grated Parmesan cheese
pinch of dried oregano

Allow 1 pita pocket per person.

Utensils

oven preheated to 350°F
knife and cutting board
mixing bowl and spoon
aluminum foil
oven mitt

Process

1. Slice the whole pita bread circle in half to make two pockets. Set aside.
2. Mix the cheeses, basil and oregano in a mixing bowl with the spoon.
3. Spoon the cheese mixture into the pita pockets.
4. Arrange the vegetables of choice in the pita pocket so they bulge out of the pocket like a flower arrangement or bouquet.
5. Carefully wrap the pita sandwich in aluminum foil.
6. Place the pita sandwich in the oven and bake for 10 minutes.
7. Wear an oven mitt and remove the pita pocket bouquet from the oven. Carefully tear open the foil and remove the sandwich. Be careful — it may be hot. Cool for several minutes.
8. Transfer to a lunch plate.
9. Eat the pita pocket bouquet with fingers or a fork.

Frankly Flowers

Serves 5 to 8

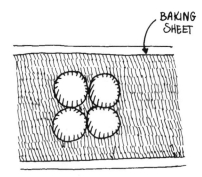

BAKING SHEET

CUT IN HALF

HOT DOG

X

TOP

SIDE

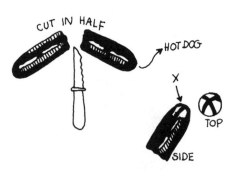

HOT DOG

SEEDS

DOUGH BALL

Ingredients

nonstick cooking spray
4 frankfurters or hot dogs
sesame or poppy seeds

1 loaf frozen white bread dough
honey
mustard or ketchup in squeeze bottles

Utensils

oven preheated to 350°F
kitchen knife
oven mitt
tray

baking sheets
pastry brush
doily

Process

1. Spray a light coating of cooking spray on the baking sheets.
2. Cut bread dough into equal slices about ¼ inch wide with a knife. Cut each slice into 4 equal pieces.
3. Roll each piece of dough into a ball.
4. Place the four balls on the baking sheet in a cluster so that they touch one another. Continue cutting the dough, rolling it into balls and arranging the balls on the baking sheet in clusters of four. Each group of four balls of dough should be at least 1 inch from the other groupings. Set aside.
5. Cut frankfurters in half crosswise. Cut a ¼ to ½-inch deep X through the round ends of frankfurters, but do not cut the frankfurter in pieces — just make some slashes. See illustrations.
6. Place the frankfurters with the slashes facing upward in the centers of each of the dough ball clusters. These will become flower shapes when baked.
7. Bake the frankfurter flowers in the oven for 15 to 20 minutes. Wear an oven mitt and remove the frankfurter flowers from the oven. Let cool for a few minutes.
8. Next, dip the pastry brush in the honey and brush the bread of the flowers. Sprinkle some seeds on the bread flowers. The honey will cause them to stick.
9. Squeeze mustard or ketchup on the flowers, if desired, before serving. Serve the Frankly Flowers on a doily-covered tray with the flowers arranged like a spring bouquet.

Chapter 8

Earth, Sea & Sky

Gulps from Outer Space

Serves 10 or more

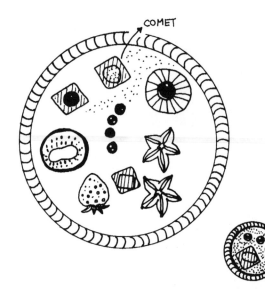

Ingredients

choice of fruits, such as

| kiwi fruit | peaches | nectarines |
| strawberries | prunes | cherries |

2 large bottles dark purple concord grape juice

Utensils

knife and cutting board
ice cube tray
punch bowl, large pitcher or clear bowl
cups and spoons

STAR FRUIT

Process

1. Cut some fruit into chunks.
2. Put a chunk of fruit in each ice cube tray compartment.
3. Pour enough juice over the fruit in the ice cube tray to cover the fruit. These cubes might represent ice-covered comets.
4. Place ice cube trays in the freezer. When the comets are almost frozen, pour the grape juice in the punch bowl (to represent outer space).
5. Remove the frozen comets from the ice cube trays and add them to the punch.
6. Next look at the other fruit choices and decide which will represent planets, stars and other objects in outer space. For example, a cherry surrounded by a pineapple circle might be Saturn, star fruit slices might be stars, kiwi fruit slices might represent Mars, blueberries might be meteors, strawberries asteroids, and for imagination, other fruits might be aliens from other worlds. Add these fruits to the punch. They will float on the grape juice like planets floating in space.
7. Ladle the punch and the fruits into cups to serve and enjoy.
▲ Serve the punch with spoons so the fruit can be eaten with spoons and will not pose a choking hazard.

Forest Floor Fallen Logs

Ingredients

Serves 5 to 8

1 package celery
1 small tomato
black olives
1 to 3 tablespoons mayonnaise
1 to 3 teaspoons poppy seeds
shredded lettuce or spinach leaves

1 can tuna, packed in water
1 dill pickle
4 ounces grated cheddar cheese

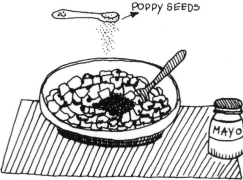

Utensils

paper towels
small bowl
small mixing bowl and spoon

sieve
knife and cutting board
flat plate

Process

1. Separate the celery stalks and wash well. Dry each piece of celery with a paper towel. Set aside.
2. Place the sieve over a bowl. Dump the can of tuna in the sieve to drain. Set aside.
3. Chop the tomato, pickle and olives into tiny pieces with a knife.
4. Mix the tuna, tomato, pickle, olives and cheese in the small mixing bowl with a mixing spoon.
5. Add 1 to 3 tablespoons of mayonnaise to the tuna mixture and stir. Add 1 to 2 teaspoons of poppy seeds to the tuna mixture and mix well.
6. Fill the grooves of a celery stalk section with a spoonful of the tuna mixture. Wipe away any excess tuna.
7. Sprinkle more of the poppy seeds on the flat plate. Dip the celery — tuna side down — in the poppy seeds. Lift the celery from the poppy seeds and place on the serving plate. The stuffed celery will look like a fallen log in the forest. The "logs" can be sliced into slabs, or eaten as entire logs.
8. Fill all the celery log sections, placing them on the serving plate after covering them with poppy seeds. Decorate around the logs with lettuce or spinach leaves.

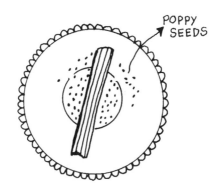

Apple Saturn Biscuit Circles

Serves 5 or more

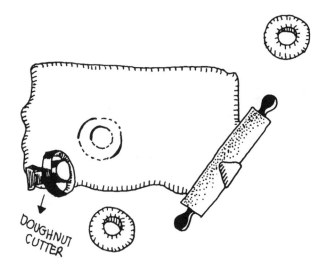

DOUGHNUT CUTTER

MELON SCOOP

Ingredients

baking mix, such as
  Bisquick
1 apple, unpeeled
butter, optional

Utensils

oven preheated to 425°F or according to package directions
rolling pin
doughnut cutter
small melon ball scoop
baking sheet
oven mitt

Process

1. Prepare biscuits according to the package directions.
2. Roll out the biscuit dough with a rolling pin.
3. Cut the biscuits with a special "doughnut cutter." A doughnut cutter has a ring with a hole in the center.
4. Put the "doughnut" biscuits on a baking sheet.
5. Push the melon ball scoop into the apple and turn to scoop out apple balls.
6. Place the apple balls in the hole of the biscuits.
7. Place the apple biscuits in the oven and bake according to package directions, usually about 8 minutes.
8. When they are baked, wear an oven mitt and remove from the oven. Cool for a few minutes.
9. Place the apple biscuits on a serving plate. Serve with butter, if desired.

Star Biscuits

 bread   bake   about 30 minutes   easiest

Ingredients

Serves 10

1 can refrigerator baking powder biscuits
flour
cold butter
honey and jam, optional

Utensils

preheat oven according to package directions
small chilled bowl
baking sheet
oven mitt

wax paper
star cookie cutter or sharp knife
melon ball scoop

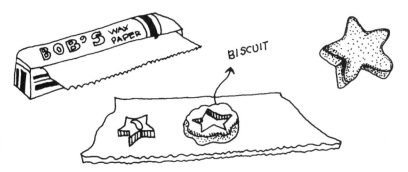

Process

1. Chill a small bowl in the refrigerator until later.
2. Pull out a large piece of wax paper and place it on the work surface.
3. Separate the biscuits and place them on the wax paper.
4. Dip the cookie cutter in flour and cut the biscuits into star shapes. If the cookie cutter is slightly larger than biscuits, gently press the dough with the palm of the hand to make biscuits larger.
▲ If a cookie cutter is unavailable, use a knife to cut a freehand star in the biscuit, and remove the unused dough.
5. Place the star biscuits on the baking sheet about 2 inches from one another. Place the left-over scraps of dough on the baking sheet to bake for additional snacks.
6. Bake the star biscuits according to package directions, usually about 8 minutes. Wear an oven mitt and remove the stars from the oven. Set aside.
7. Scoop one butter ball per biscuit from the cold butter and place in a small, chilled bowl.
8. Put the star-shaped biscuits on a round platter, and place the butter balls all around them. Serve with small dishes of honey or jam, if desired.
9. Enjoy biscuits for breakfast or any other time a warm, delicious, buttery biscuit is needed.

easiest

about 30 minutes

bake

sandwich

Baked Bumpy Roads

Serves 2 to 4

PAPER PLATE

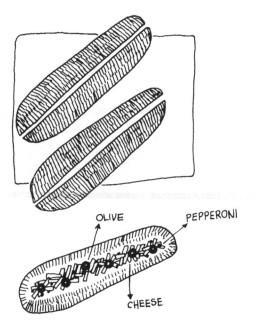

OLIVE   PEPPERONI

CHEESE

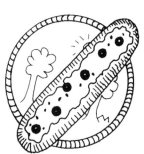

Ingredients

pepperoni
2 French rolls, each cut in half
grated mozzarella cheese

black olives
grated cheddar cheese

Utensils
oven preheated to 375°F
permanent markers
bowl and fork
oven mitt

paper plates
knife and cutting board
baking sheet

Process

1. Draw trees, houses and other outdoor designs on the paper plate with the permanent markers.
2. Cut the olives and pepperoni into small pieces with a knife.
3. Cut the 2 rolls in half so there are four pieces.
4. Place the cheddar and mozzarella cheeses in a bowl and lightly combine them with a fork.
5. Place the rolls on a baking sheet and cover each piece with a layer of the combined cheeses.
6. Arrange a layer of pepperoni bits over the cheese. Place olives on top of the pepperoni.
7. Bake the rolls for about 5 minutes or until the cheese has melted. Wear an oven mitt and remove the rolls from the oven. Let cool for several minutes. The melted toppings on the baked rolls will look like a bumpy road.
8. Place the Baked Bumpy Roads on the decorated paper plates to serve.
9. Consider serving Baked Bumpy Roads with Trees in Snow (page 86) and Cantaloupe Canoes (page 77) for an environmentally imaginative meal.

Star-Studded Pizza

entree

bake

about 45 minutes

easier

Ingredients

Serves 8 to 10

3 slices of cheese
one-half of a 3½-ounce package sliced pepperoni
prepared frozen cheese pizza

Utensils

oven preheated to 375°F or according to package directions
2-inch star-shaped cookie cutter
¾-inch star-shaped cookie cutter
baking sheet
oven mitt

Process

1. With the 2-inch star-shaped cookie cutter, cut each slice of cheese into two stars. The extra cheese trimmings can be used to decorate the pizza.
2. With a ¾-inch star-shaped cookie cutter, cut a star from each slice of pepperoni.
3. Chop any pepperoni trimmings to add to the pizza later, too.
4. Spread the pepperoni and cheese stars over the pizza. Add any extra pepperoni or cheese trimmings.
5. Place the pizza on the baking sheet.
6. Put the pizza in the oven and bake according to package directions, usually about 20 minutes or until hot and bubbly.
7. Wear an oven mitt and remove the star-studded pizza from the oven. Serve as an entree or as a party snack.

Under-the-Sea Cakes

Serves 6 to 8

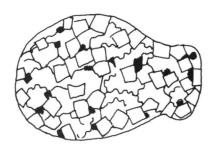

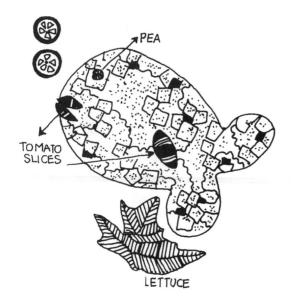

PEA

TOMATO SLICES

LETTUCE

Ingredients

1 cup dry bread crumbs

2 tablespoons butter or margarine

1 tablespoon snipped fresh chives

2 teaspoons flour

nonstick cooking spray

peas

fish-shaped crackers

leftover mashed potatoes

1 egg yolk

1 (7-ounce) can tuna in water, drained

3 eggs, beaten

1 cherry tomato, cut into slices

oyster crackers

lettuce leaves

Utensils

oven preheated to 350°F

shallow dish

oven mitt

small bowl and spoon

baking sheet

spatula

Process

1. Pour the bread crumbs on a plate. Set aside.
2. Place the mashed potatoes, butter and egg yolk in a bowl. Mix well with a spoon. Add the chives and drained tuna to the mashed potato mixture. Mix again.
3. Divide the tuna and potato mixture into 6 equal portions. Place some flour on hands and shape the 6 tuna portions into flat pear shapes. Shape the thinner end of the pear shapes to form a V-shape patty or cake, like a fish's tail. See illustrations. Or, feel free to design any fish shapes you can imagine, keeping them fairly rounded so they will hold together when baking.
4. Place the beaten eggs into a shallow dish.
5. Gently add the fish-shaped cakes to the egg and carefully turn them over and over, covering the top and bottom of the cake with the egg mixture. Then, coat fish cakes in bread crumbs and place them on the baking sheet. Spray a light coating of cooking spray on each fish cake.
6. Bake the fish cakes for 20 to 25 minutes. Wear an oven mitt and remove the fish cakes from the oven. Transfer the fish cakes with a spatula to individual plates.
7. Garnish each fish with features made with the remaining foods to create a mouth, gills and a tail. Tomato slices are fun to use as bubbles leading from each fish's mouth. Add some oyster and fish crackers to make additional bubbles or underwater life and some lettuce as seaweed.
8. Serve hot as the main part of a meal or on a platter for a fun-time party snack.

Erupting Lava Apple

Ingredients

Allow 1 apple per person

1 apple per person

¼ cup peanut butter per apple

⅛ cup dried fruit bits or seeds, such as

    raisins   sunflower seeds

    dried mixed fruits   popcorn

▲ recipe also works well with softened cheddar cheese

Utensils

apple corer

small bowls

butter knife

Process

1. Remove the core of the apple with the apple coring tool. Discard the core with seeds.
2. Mix the peanut butter and the fruit bits or seeds in one of the small bowls. Stir them together with a butter knife.
3. Fill the hole in the apple with the peanut butter and fruit bits mixture.
4. Sprinkle more fruit or seeds on top of the apple.
5. Eat the lava apple for a snack. The lava will spread and erupt over your chin and face. Napkins will help keep the lava under control.

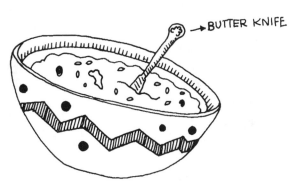

BUTTER KNIFE

FRUIT BITS + PEANUT BUTTER

easiest | 10 to 15 minutes | snack

Apple Galaxy

Serves 1 to 2

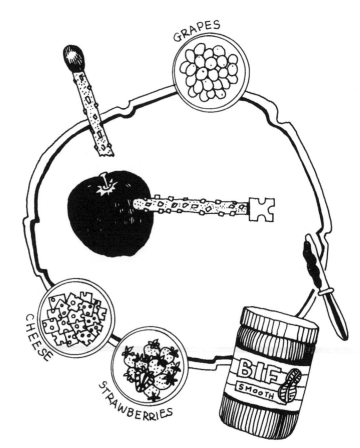

GRAPES

CHEESE

STRAWBERRIES

BIF SMOOTH

Ingredients

apple
pretzel sticks
selection of foods, such as
    cheese cubes, carrot slices, celery slices, broccoli florets
selection of firm fruits, such as
    blueberries, raisins, grapes, strawberries
mini-marshmallows, optional
peanut butter, optional

Utensils

knife and cutting board   several bowls
metal skewer   fork
toothpicks

Process

1. Wash and dry the apple.
2. Place choices of foods in individual bowls.
3. Carefully poke a few holes in the apple with the skewer.
4. Push a pretzel stick into a cheese cube.
5. Push the other end of the pretzel stick into one of the poked holes in the apple.
6. Press other foods onto pretzel sticks and then into the apple.
7. Dip fruits into peanut butter and stick them on the apple, if desired.
8. The apple will be covered with foods projecting from it, resembling planets and stars revolving in a galaxy.
9. Place the apple galaxy on the table for a fun-time snack.

Cooking Art

Treasure Lake Pudding

Ingredients

Serves 4

items for "buried treasure" in the pudding, such as

broken cookies	fresh fruit or bits of dried fruit
miniature marshmallows	chocolate chips
peanut butter	nuts

2 cups cold milk

1 package (4 serving size) instant pudding, any favorite flavor

Utensils

measuring spoons

4 dessert dishes

measuring cup

1-quart shaker with a tight lid

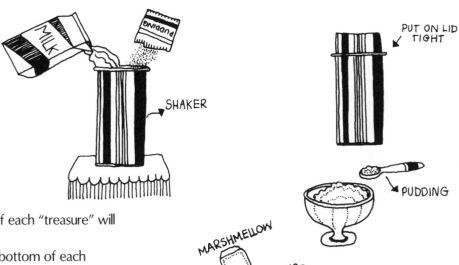

Process

1. Choose four different "treasures" to bury in the pudding. A teaspoon of each "treasure" will be about right.
2. Put a teaspoon of one of the four different types of "treasures" in the bottom of each dessert dish. Each dish will have a different treasure. Set aside.
3. Pour 2 cups of cold milk into the shaker. Add the pudding mix.
4. Put the lid on shaker very tightly.
5. Shake very hard for at least 45 seconds. Open the shaker.
6. Gently spoon or pour some pudding from the shaker over the treasures in each dish.
7. The pudding will thicken quickly and be ready to eat in 5 minutes. Put the pudding in the refrigerator if it is not eaten immediately.
8. Serve the pudding with hidden buried treasures in it as a delightful dessert with a different surprise for everyone.

easier   about 30 minutes   dessert

Constellation Stencil Cake

Serves 8 to 16

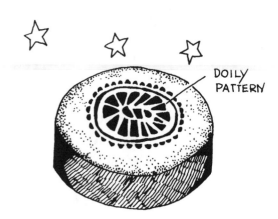

DOILY
PATTERN

Ingredients

prebaked round chocolate cake without icing
⅛ cup confectioners' sugar

Utensils

paper and scissors   doily, optional
spoon   sifter
thin paper plates, any color, optional

Process

1. Place the round cake layer on a plate.
2. Cut stars out of paper and place the paper stars on the surface of the cake. Consider placing the stars in an actual constellation pattern such as Orion or the Big Dipper.
3. Spoon the confectioners' sugar into the sifter.
4. Hold the sifter over the cake and sift the confectioners' sugar generously over the top of the cake and the star patterns.
5. Remove the paper stars. Be careful not to spill too much of the confectioners' sugar from the stars on the cake or the stencil design will be blurred.
6. When the star patterns are removed, a constellation pattern appears on the cake.
7. For additional decoration, cut thin paper plates into star shapes.
8. Cut the constellation cake with a cake knife and place individual servings on the star-shaped paper plates.

▲ Instead of stars, carefully place a paper doily on top of cake.

Chapter 9

My Body & Yours

Scoopy the Salad

Serves 1

Ingredients

lettuce
about 1 cup cottage cheese
selection of favorite fresh, raw vegetables, such as

cherry tomatoes	alfalfa sprouts	green bell pepper slices
olives	broccoli	red bell pepper slices
zucchini slices	peas	beans

Utensils

plate
ice-cream scoop

Process

1. Place a lettuce leaf on a plate.
2. Place a scoop of cottage cheese on the lettuce with the ice-cream scoop.
3. Decorate the cottage cheese with the vegetables to design a face, animal, character or colorful design.
4. Serve immediately or place in the refrigerator until serving time as a salad or light lunch.
▲ This recipe can be doubled or extended easily to serve more people. It is also delicious when made with fruit instead of vegetables.

Bread Braids

bread

bake

1 hour or more

easy

Ingredients

½ package yeast
½ tablespoon sugar
2 cups flour plus extra
butter

1 cup warm water
½ teaspoon salt
nonstick cooking spray
honey

Utensils

oven preheated to 400°F
large mixing bowl
cookie sheet

medium mixing bowl
plastic wrap

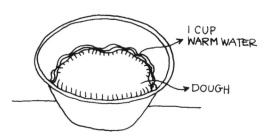

I CUP WARM WATER

DOUGH

Process

1. Dissolve the yeast in warm water in a medium mixing bowl. Let sit for 5 minutes. Add the sugar, salt and flour to the yeast mixture and mix with hands until the dough is well mixed.
2. Sprinkle about 1 tablespoon of flour on a work surface. Put the dough on the floured work surface. Knead until smooth.
3. Spray cooking spray on the inside of the large mixing bowl. Place the dough in the bowl. Cover the bowl with plastic wrap and put the bowl in a warm place. Let the dough rise until it doubles in bulk (about 1½ to 2 hours).
4. After the dough has doubled, punch it down, leaving it in the bowl to double again, about ½ hour.

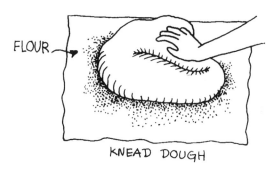

FLOUR

KNEAD DOUGH

To braid the dough ropes

▲ A note about braiding: The following description tells how to braid. However, feel free to braid in any creative design imagined.

1. Divide the dough into three equal parts. Roll the 3 dough parts into long ropes.
2. Lay the three long ropes in a line next to one another on the work surface.
3. Take the top of the ends of the ropes and pinch them together until they stick and are joined and hold well. Then, spread out the bottom sections of the rope so they fan outward.

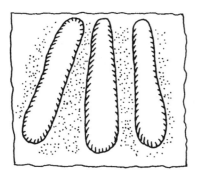   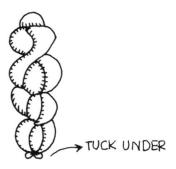

→ TUCK UNDER

4. Beginning at the top, take the rope on the right and lay it across the middle rope.

5. Continuing from the top, take the rope on the left and lay it over the rope just positioned, which is now the middle rope. (This makes all of the ropes change their original positions.)

6. Continue braiding by selecting the rope closest to the top and weaving it over the present middle rope.

7. When there is only a little rope left to braid, stop and tuck the ends under the braided loaf. Pinch to hold, if you like.

8. Spray the baking sheet with cooking spray and put the braided dough on the cookie sheet. Spray the braided dough with the cooking spray, too.

9. Bake the braid at 400°F for 30 minutes, until it is browned and makes a hollow sound when tapped with a knife handle. Remove the braid from the oven and serve on a bread board or large plate.

▲ The fragrance of fresh baking bread should have brought everyone into the kitchen by now. Each hungry person can pull off pieces of fresh bread, spread with a little butter or honey, and devour.

Veggie Folks

vegetable   about 30 minutes   easier

Ingredients

1 eggplant per veggie person
choice of cut raw vegetables, such as

carrots	zucchini	green peppers
mushrooms	sprouts	celery
carrot curls	broccoli or cauliflower	

choice of vegetable dip, such as

garbanzo bean spread   baba ganouj dip (page 88)
homemade peanut butter (page 124)   cream cheese mixed with powdered dip mix

Utensils

kitchen towel	knife and cutting board
toothpicks	dish for dip

Process

1. Wash and dry all vegetables.
▲ One eggplant will be the main body of each of the Veggie Folks.
2. Use toothpicks to attach vegetable traits and features to the eggplant body.
   Here are some suggestions for creating "Veggie Folks":
   ✔ toothpicks placed on each side of the eggplant could be arms
   ✔ add a vegetable at the end of the toothpicks to further create arms
   ✔ for hair attach carrot curls or sprouts
   ✔ eyes could be carrot circles or mushrooms
   ✔ legs could be celery sticks or long, sliced zucchini halves.
3. Continue constructing the person until all of the features are finished.
4. Place one or more Veggie Folks on the table to use as a centerpiece.
5. Fill the dip dish with the vegetable dip or spread of your choice.
6. When ready, the vegetables can be detached one by one from the centerpiece, then dipped in the dip, and eaten as a party snack.
▲ Remove the toothpicks before eating the veggies.

Serves 2 to 4 people as an appetizer

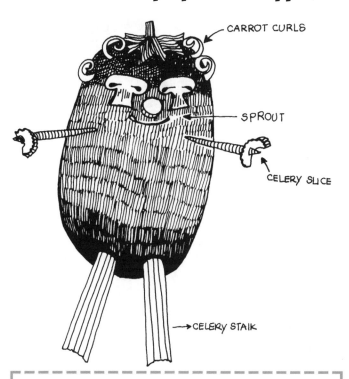

CARROT CURLS

SPROUT

CELERY SLICE

CELERY STAIK

Garbanzo Bean Spread

1 can garbanzo beans
1 clove garlic
juice from 1 lemon
1 green onion
1 T. fresh parsley
salt and pepper

Blend the above ingreidients in a blender or food processor.

easier about 30 minutes breakfast

Me and My Shadow Toast

Serves 2 to 4

Ingredients

6 slices day old bread
3 tablespoons milk
choose any toppings, such as

jam	fruit syrup
fresh berries	raisins
brown sugar	currants

3 to 4 large eggs
3 tablespoons butter

maple syrup
peanut butter
powdered sugar

Utensils

oven preheated to 150°F
shallow dish
wide frying pan
spatula

people-shaped cookie cutters or sharp knife
whisk
cooking fork

Process

1. Put a serving plate in the oven to keep warm for later.
2. Place the bread on the work surface. Press a people-shaped cookie cutter into the bread and twist a little, or cut out a person from the bread with a sharp knife.
3. Remove the cookie cutter and take the people shape out of the bread, keeping both the shape and the outline intact. Set aside. Save the scrap outline of bread.
4. Crack open 4 eggs into the shallow dish. Discard the shells. Add 3 tablespoons of milk to the eggs and whisk together.
5. Put the butter in the frying pan. Warm over medium heat to melt.
6. Dip the people shapes in the egg mixture, coating each side. Then, place the egg coated people shapes in the warm pan and cook them on each side until golden brown. Transfer the people shapes with a spatula from the pan to the warm serving plate. Leave in the warm oven.
7. Next, coat the bread scrap outlines with egg and cook them to make Shadow Toast. For additional fun, pour some of the egg mixture into the frame of the Shadow Toast to fill the hole. Cook on one side, and then turn to cook the other side until brown.
8. When the French toast is cooked, place the shadows on the warm serving plate with the people. Place the plate with Me and My Shadow Toast on the table. Each person can add toppings to their toast to decorate it and to make it even more delicious and friendly.

Cooking Art

Mix 'n Match Sandwich Faces

Allow 2 sandwich halves per person

Ingredients

two kinds of bread, such as wheat, white, sourdough, rye
choice of sandwich fillings, such as egg salad, tuna salad, peanut butter, cheese
choice of additional foods for decorating and facial features, such as

raisins	carrot pieces	green pepper pieces
celery slices	egg slices	almonds
seeds	olives	mushroom slices
cheese shapes	radish slices	apple pieces
parsley leaves	lettuce	mustard
ketchup		

Utensils

circle cookie cutter, optional
tools to cut or design foods for decorations, such as

knife	small circle cutter	vegetable peeler
apple corer	toothpicks	fork

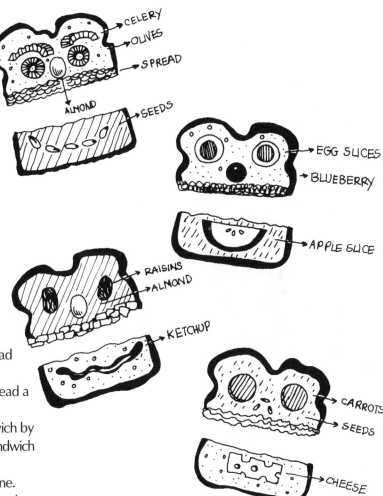

Process

1. Choose two pieces of bread for each sandwich. Cut out a circle from each slice of bread with a large circle cookie cutter, if you like, or use the bread as is.

2. Slice each piece of bread in half, making a rectangle or a semi-circle. See illustration. Spread a sandwich filling on the bread. Top with a matching type and shape of bread.

3. Select from the decorating foods to design eyes and nose on the top half of the sandwich by pressing foods into the bread. In the same way, design a mouth on the other half of the sandwich for the lower part of the face (sandwich).

4. For the fun part, first place all the eye and nose sandwich halves on a serving tray in a line. Then, place the mouth sandwich halves beneath each eye and nose half, but do not match the bread types. Place miss-matched halves together so the faces will be all mixed up.

5. Everyone chooses a top half and a bottom half that they like that matches or does not match and places it on their own sandwich plate. What a crazy mixed up lunch!

Family Pizza

Allow 1 pizza shape for each family member

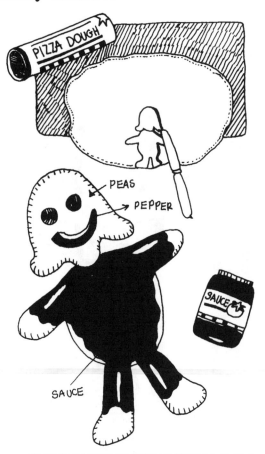

PIZZA DOUGH

PEAS

PEPPER

SAUCE

Each family member can choose to eat his own pizza shape or to gobble up another family member for lunch or dinner!

Ingredients

refrigerated pizza dough
vegetable oil
canned pizza sauce
favorite foods to design and individualize each pizza, such as

cheese, shredded or cut in shapes	onion
sliced pepperoni	large button mushrooms
red, orange or yellow bell pepper	hot dog circles
pineapple chunks	tomato slices or wedges
sliced or chopped olives	green peas

Utensils

oven preheated to 425°F	teaspoon
pastry brush	knife or kitchen scissors
baking sheet	oven mitt
spatula	

Process

1. Open the package of refrigerated pizza dough and spread the dough out on the work surface.
2. Use a knife to draw the outline of a body shape, each resembling a family member. Then, cut the shape out and place it on a baking sheet.
3. Brush a teaspoon of vegetable oil on the pizza dough.
4. Create other family members. Place them on the baking sheet and brush oil over each of them.
5. Use remaining foods to create clothes, features and decorations on the family member dough shapes with pizza sauce.
6. Add additional design with cheese, peas, mushrooms, bell peppers and other foods of choice. Cut, shape or arrange the foods as desired to enhance the pizza family's individual features.
7. Place the pizza family in the oven and bake for 10 to 12 minutes, until edges are browned and cheese is bubbly. Wear an oven mitt and remove the pizza family from the oven. Let cool for a few minutes before serving with spatula.

Cooking Art

Scary Eyeballs

Ingredients

Serves 6 to 12

6 hard-boiled eggs
1 tablespoon prepared mustard
¼ teaspoon salt
alfalfa sprouts

2 tablespoons mayonnaise
1 tablespoon sweet pickle relish
6 black or green olives

Utensils

knife and cutting board
fork
1 Styrofoam egg carton, washed with soapy water and dried

medium bowl
spoon

Process

1. Crack open a hard-boiled egg. Peel the shell from the egg.
2. Cut the egg in half the short way across the middle, not from end to end.
3. Remove cooked yolk from the egg and place it in the bowl. Repeat cracking, peeling and cutting the other hard-boiled eggs.
4. Mash all the yolks with a fork. Add mayonnaise, mustard, pickle relish and salt to the yolks and mix well.
5. Spoon yolk mixture into each egg white half to resemble an eyeball.
6. Slice each olive in half with a knife.
7. Place an olive on top of each egg to resemble the pupil and iris of an eye.
8. Stuff each egg carton compartment with alfalfa sprouts. Place an eyeball on top of the sprouts in each egg carton compartment.
9. To serve, place the egg carton on the table so guests can select eyeballs to munch.

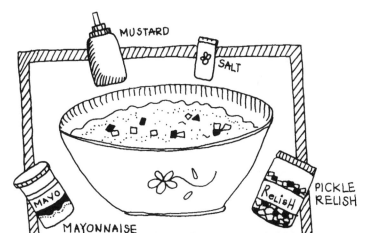

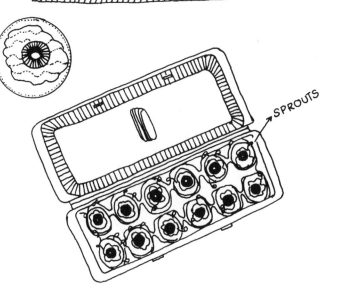

Funny Fingers

Serves 2 or more

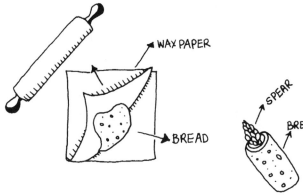

WAX PAPER

BREAD

SPEAR

BREAD

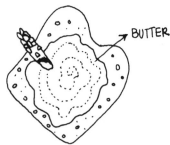

BUTTER

Ingredients

can of asparagus spears
white bread
butter

Utensils

oven preheated to 350°F
knife and cutting board
rolling pin
baking sheet
clean gloves

can opener
wax paper
spreading knife
oven mitt
scissors

Process

1. Open the can of asparagus spears with the can opener. Pour the water out of the can to drain. Carefully take the asparagus spears out of the can, trying not to break them.
2. Count the number of spears. Set out the same number of bread slices as asparagus spears.
3. Cut off all bread crusts with a knife.
4. Place one slice of bread between two sheets of wax paper.
5. Flatten the bread with a rolling pin. Peel the bread from the wax paper.
6. Butter one side of the bread. Then, with buttered side down, place one asparagus spear on the bread with the tip sticking out one end. Roll the asparagus spear in the bread. Place the rolled bread and asparagus spear on a baking sheet.
7. Place the asparagus spear bread in the oven and bake for 10 minutes. Wear an oven mitt and remove the asparagus spears from the oven. Set aside to cool.
8. Cut the fingers off the clean gloves. Place the asparagus fingers in the sections where the glove fingers have been cut away. Place on a plate and serve the silly asparagus fingers for an outrageous lunch or frightening party snack.

Smiley Snack

Ingredients

Serves 2 to 5

1 to 5 red apples
¼ cup peanut butter
choice of food items for "teeth", such as
   miniature marshmallows, berries, raisins, white (or other) cooked beans, peas
squirt can of cheese, optional
sliced fruits or other foods, such as

tomato slices	kiwi fruit	cherries or strawberries
olives	orange slices	banana circles

Utensils

knife and cutting board
spreading knife

Process

1. Cut the apple into quarters with a knife.
2. Cut each quarter in half again to make two thin slices for each "smile."
3. Spread peanut butter on one side of each thin smiley-slice to act as a glue.
4. Choose the foods that will be the teeth of the smile. Arrange the teeth foods — marshmallows, berries, raisins, other foods or any combination of them — on the peanut butter.
5. Assemble the second apple slice with the peanut butter slice facing down on top of the first slice and the "teeth." This forms a mouth with teeth inside.
6. Decorate other features around each smile, if desired, by using any remaining ingredients.
7. Serve the smiley faces on a cheerful plate as a snack.
8. Read funny books or tell funny jokes while eating.

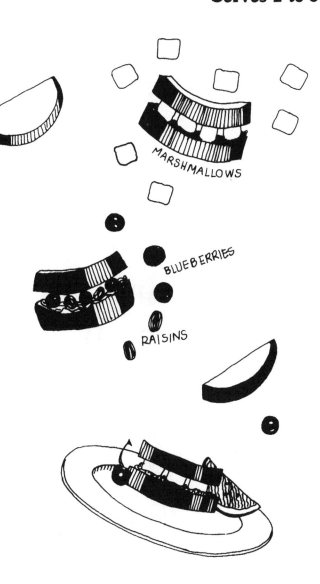

MARSHMALLOWS

BLUEBERRIES

RAISINS

easy   about 45 minutes   bake   dessert

Molasses People Cookies

Serves 8 to 10

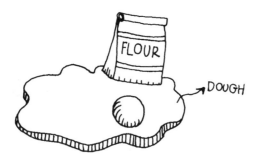

DOUGH

FLATTEN BALL

Ingredients

4 tablespoons sugar
2 tablespoons vegetable oil
2⅓ cups flour
½ teaspoon salt
½ teaspoon ginger
colored squeeze icing

½ cup molasses
2 tablespoons milk
½ teaspoon baking soda
1 teaspoon cinnamon
nonstick cooking spray

Utensils

oven preheated to 350°F
several large bowls
flour sifter
flat-bottom glass, optional

measuring cups and spoons
wooden mixing spoon
baking sheet
spatula

Process

1. Measure the sugar, molasses, vegetable oil and milk into a large bowl. Mix together with a spoon.
2. Measure ¼ cup flour. Set aside for the kneading in step four.
3. Place the remaining flour, baking soda, salt, cinnamon and ginger in the flour sifter and sift into a bowl. After sifting the ingredients, dump them in the molasses mixture and mix well.
4. Work the dough with hands until smooth. If it is too soft, add a little more flour; if too crumbly, add a little more milk. The dough should make a ball that holds together well.
5. To model people, begin with two balls — a large one for the body and a smaller one for the head. Flatten them with the palm of the hand or a flat-bottom glass. Add arms, legs, facial features and clothing with bits of dough as desired.
6. Spray the baking sheet with cooking spray. Place each Molasses People Cookie on the baking sheet.
7. Bake the cookies in the oven for 10 minutes. Wear an oven mitt and remove them from the oven. Let cool for a few minutes, then transfer the cookies from the baking sheet to a plate using a spatula.
8. Use the squeeze icing to design and paint features on the cookies, if desired.
9. Serve when ready as a warm, friendly dessert or snack.

Chapter 10

Animals & Creatures

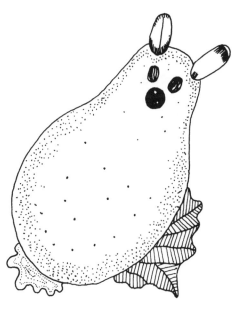

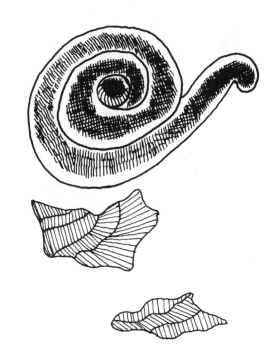

easiest

about 30 minutes

bake

bread

Dinosaur Claws

Serves 5

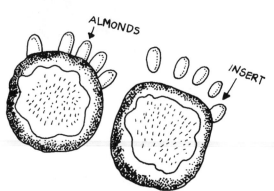
ADD MARGARINE
← CINNAMON SUGAR

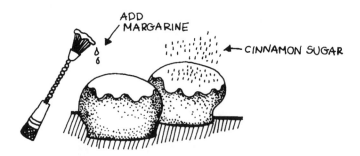
ALMONDS
INSERT

Ingredients

1 can of refrigerator biscuits
margarine, melted
cinnamon sugar
almond slivers

Utensils

oven preheated to 425°F or according to package directions
baking sheet
pastry brush
oven mitt
squares of plain cardboard
permanent markers

Process

1. Open the package of biscuits.
2. Place the biscuits on the baking sheet.
3. Place the biscuits in the oven and bake according to package directions, usually about 8 to 10 minutes.
4. Wear an oven mitt and remove the baking sheet and biscuits from the oven.
5. Brush each biscuit with melted margarine. Sprinkle biscuits with cinnamon sugar.
6. While the biscuit is still very warm, carefully insert 5 almond slivers around the edge of the biscuit so it looks like the claws of a dinosaur.
7. Draw tracks on the squares of cardboard with the permanent markers.
8. Serve the claws on the cardboard squares.

Cooking Art

Snail Bread

Ingredients

Serves 10

nonstick cooking spray
2 cups bread flour
1 package active dry yeast
1 tablespoon vegetable oil
dried currants

1¼ cups warm water
2 cups whole wheat flour, plus extra
pinch of salt
2 teaspoons honey
ground brown cookie crumbs

Utensils

oven preheated to 350°F
baking sheet
large bowl and spoon
plastic wrap

measuring cups and spoons
2 small bowls and spoon
pastry brush
oven mitts

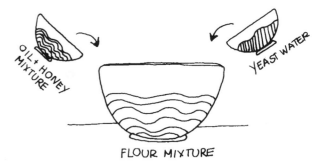

FLOUR MIXTURE

Process

1. Spray a light coating of cooking spay on the baking sheet.
2. Place 1 cup of warm water in a small bowl. Add the yeast to the water and mix. Set aside.
3. In a large bowl, mix the flour and salt together. Add the yeast water to the flour mixture and mix well. Set aside.
4. Place the vegetable oil, honey and ¼ cup water into a bowl and mix well. Pour the oil and honey mixture in the flour mixture and blend until a stiff dough is formed.
5. Sprinkle 2 tablespoons flour onto the work surface. Take the dough out of the bowl and place it on the floured surface and knead.
6. Divide the dough into 20 pieces. Roll each dough piece into a rope shape about 4 inches long and 1 inch around. Brush one side of the rope with water.
7. Start at one end of the rope and wind a coil using most of the dough. This will be the snail's coiled shell. Turn the other end of the dough into a hook shape for the snail's head.
8. Place the snail on the baking sheet. Make additional snails or experiment making different animals with the remaining dough.
9. Place the snails in the oven and bake until golden brown. Wear an oven mitt and take the baking sheet out of the oven.
10. Remove the snail from the baking sheet with a spatula. Sprinkle some cookie crumbs on the plate. Place the snails on the cookie crumbs to serve.

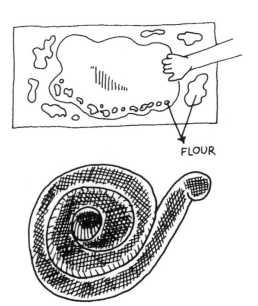

FLOUR

Bunny Pears

Serves 4 to 6

Ingredients

1 can pear halves
lettuce leaves
selection of foods, such as
    toasted almonds
    strawberries
    raisins
    blueberries
squirt can of whipped cream, optional

Utensils

can opener
strainer
plate

Process

1. Open the can of pears with a can opener.
2. Place the pear halves into a strainer to drain over the sink.
3. Arrange the lettuce leaves on a plate.
4. Place the pear halves, rounded side up, on the lettuce leaves.
5. Use the remaining ingredients to add features to each pear to make it into a bunny.
6. If desired, just before serving, squirt a whipped cream tail on the bunny.

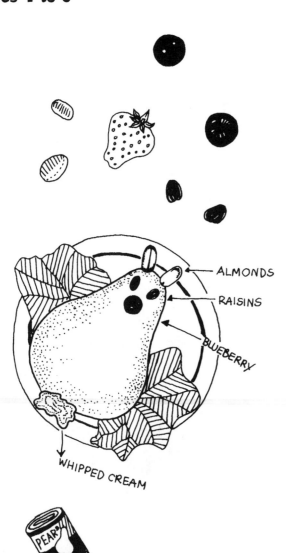

ALMONDS
RAISINS
BLUEBERRY
WHIPPED CREAM

Puppy in a Blanket

Ingredients

Serves 8

1 sheet frozen pastry dough, such as Pepperidge Farm
nonstick cooking spray
2 tablespoons milk
mustard, ketchup, cheese slices, optional

8 hot dogs
sesame or poppy seeds

Utensils

oven preheated to 350°F
knife and cutting board
oven mitt

baking sheet
pastry brush
spatula

Process

1. Spray a light coating of cooking spay on the surface of the baking sheet.
2. Cut the 8 hot dogs in half so there are 16 "puppies."
3. Open the package of pastry dough and unfold one sheet. Cut the sheet of dough into 16 equal rectangles long enough to cover half a hot dog each. Save any remaining dough.
4. Place each puppy on the baking sheet about 6 inches apart from one another. Put a rectangle of dough on top of each puppy to make a blanket.
5. Cut out designs, initials, pictures or shapes with a knife from the remaining dough to decorate the blankets. Brush the backs of the shapes with milk and place them on the puppy blankets to make a design on each blanket.
6. Brush the blankets with a pastry brush dipped in milk. Sprinkle each blanket with sesame or poppy seeds, if desired.
7. Place the Puppies in Blankets in the oven and bake for 10 to 15 minutes until golden. Wear an oven mitt and remove the pups from the oven. Let cool.
8. Use a spatula to remove the puppies and blankets from the baking sheet and serve on a large platter.
9. Serve plain or accompanied with dishes of mustard, ketchup or cheese slices for a party lunch or as part of a meal.

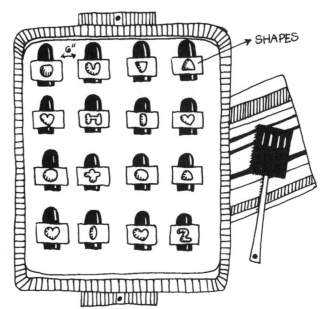

SHAPES

Animals & Creatures

Mr. P. B. Grrr...Ape

**Serves 8 to 10 or more —
1 or 2 sandwiches per person**

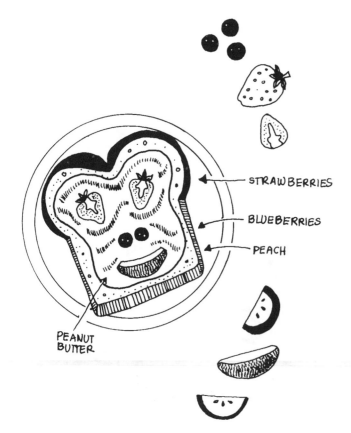

STRAWBERRIES

BLUEBERRIES

PEACH

PEANUT BUTTER

Ingredients

4 cups roasted peanuts in the shell (makes 2 cups when shelled)
2 tablespoons of cooking oil
4 tablespoons of honey
salt, to taste
selection of fresh fruits, such as

| bananas | grapes | peaches |
| strawberries | blueberries | apples |

sliced bread

Utensils

bowl or container	food processor or blender
measuring cups and spoons	spatula
container with snap-on lid, or a bowl	knife and cutting board
spreading knife	rubber spatula

Process

1. Shell the peanuts and place them in a container or bowl.
2. Measure two cups of shelled peanuts into the food processor or blender. Add the cooking oil, honey and salt.
3. Put on the lid and blend or process until the peanut mixture becomes peanut butter. For chunky style, stop processing while chunks are left. For creamy style, process until peanut butter is completely smooth.
4. Use the rubber spatula to scoop the peanut butter from the processor into a plastic container with a snap-on lid for storage later.
5. Select fruits to decorate the face of an open-faced sandwich that may look like an ape or any other type of face. Cut the fruits with a knife into chunks, slices, wedges or circles.
6. Place a slice of bread on a plate. Spread P. B. (peanut butter) on the slice of bread.
7. Add fruit decorations to design Mr. P. B. Grrr...Ape. Other creative faces or designs are also fun.
8. Serve the open-faced sandwich for lunch or snack, but don't "monkey" around. It's a jungle out there!
9. Store extra peanut butter in the refrigerator.

Prehistoric Eggs

Ingredients

Serves 4 to 6

4 to 6 eggs
cool water
1 tablespoon food coloring (choose more than one color if desired)
lettuce

Utensils

saucepan
bowl
metal spoon

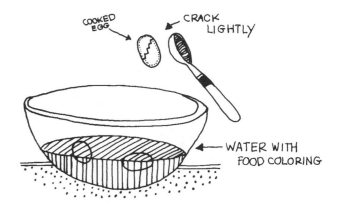

COOKED EGG   CRACK LIGHTLY

← WATER WITH FOOD COLORING

Process

1. Place the eggs in a saucepan filled with cool water on the stove.
2. Bring the eggs to a boil over medium heat. Turn heat down and gently simmer the eggs for 8 to 10 minutes. Then, take the pan off the heat.
3. Fill a bowl with cool water. Add several drops of food coloring to the water and mix. For more than one color, add drops of food coloring to several bowls of water.
4. Put the eggs in the bowl of colored water, or a few eggs in each bowl of different colored water.
5. One at a time, lift each egg out of the water and carefully crack the shells all over with the back of a spoon. Do not peel any of the eggshell off yet.
6. Return the eggs to the colored water until cool.
7. Next, take the eggs out of the water with the spoon. Peel the cracked eggs.
8. Place the lettuce in the serving bowl to resemble grass or weeds. Place the prehistoric eggs on the lettuce to serve.
9. Eat as a snack or part of a meal.

PEEL

Banana Snake

Serves 1 to 2 per snake

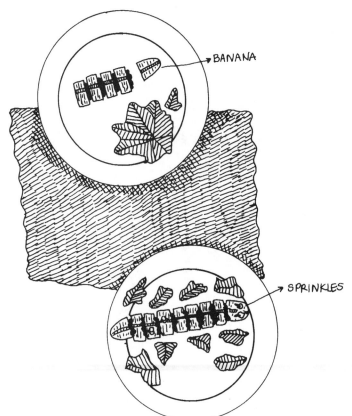

BANANA

SPRINKLES

Ingredients

lettuce
peanut butter
chow mien noodles
banana
raisins
sprinkles, bread crumbs, small candies

Utensils

plates
table knife

Process

1. Tear a lettuce leaf into small pieces and place on a plate.
2. Slice the banana into ½-inch chunks.
3. Smear peanut butter on the cut sides of the banana chunks.
4. Place the peanut buttery banana slices in a row on the plate. Add the ends of the bananas to form the ends of the snake. The sections will stick together with the peanut butter.
5. Place a small dab of peanut butter where the eyes and spots are on the snake. The peanut butter will act as glue. Add sprinkles or candies as the eyes, etc.
6. Decorate the snake by sticking on other ingredients using the peanut butter.
7. Enjoy as an entertaining snack or dessert.

Animal Cheese Crackers

snack   bake   about 45 minutes   easy

Ingredients

Serves 4 to 8

nonstick cooking spray
½ teaspoon mustard powder
½ cup shredded sharp cheddar cheese

1 cup all-purpose flour, plus extra
¼ cup butter, chilled
1 egg

Utensils

oven preheated to 350°F
sifter
butter knife
measuring spoons
animal cookie cutters
oven mitt

2 baking sheets
2 mixing bowls
whisk
rolling pin
pastry brush

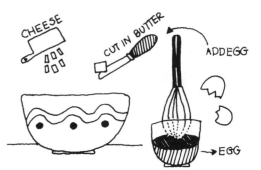

Process

1. Spray a light coating of cooking spray on both baking sheets.
2. Hold the sifter over a mixing bowl. Measure the flour and mustard into the sifter and sift them into the bowl.
3. Cut the butter into the flour mixture with the knife, forming pea-size pieces of dough. Do not mix. Mix the cheese into the flour mixture by lightly tossing the ingredients together.
4. Break the egg into a different bowl. Discard the shell and beat the egg with a whisk. Add 2 tablespoons of the beaten egg to the cheese and flour mixture. Work the egg, cheese and flour together by hand to form a smooth dough. Then, transfer the dough to a floured work surface and knead well.
5. Rub a little flour on the rolling pin and roll out the dough to about 1 inch thick.
6. Press a cookie cutter into the dough and gently cut and remove the dough shape from the rest of the dough. Place it on a baking sheet. Continue cutting shapes from the dough until most of the dough is used. There will be dough left over. Mold it into a ball and then roll it out for cutting with cookie cutters until all the dough is used.
7. Brush the tops of the animal cracker shapes with the remaining beaten egg. Sprinkle with sesame seeds, if desired.
8. Bake the animal crackers for 12 to 15 minutes at 350°F until golden. Remove the crackers from the oven wearing an oven mitt. Let the crackers cool on the baking sheet.
9. Transfer the crackers to a serving plate for a party treat, snack or to serve with a cup of tomato soup for lunch.

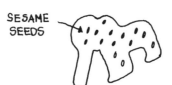

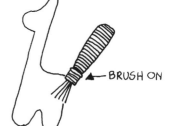

easiest

about 30 minutes

dessert

Scooper Sculpture

Allow 1 creature per person

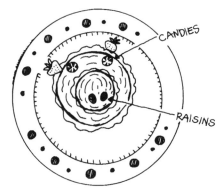

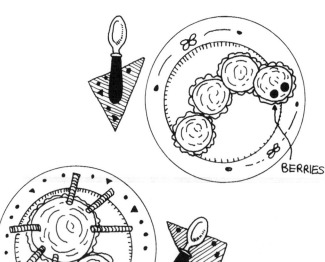

Ingredients

different flavors of ice cream, frozen hard (strawberry is effective for pigs, chocolate for
bears, mint for frogs and so on)
selection of favorite decorations, such as

chocolate kisses	strawberries/berries	almonds
raisins	cinnamon candies	chocolate chips
sliced fruits	M & M's	long shoelace licorice

Utensils

large ice-cream scoop   small ice-cream scoop
cold plate   spreading knife

Process

1. Imagine an original creature to create with scoops of ice cream. For example, a snake could
   be several scoops of ice cream in a row, a piglet could be two strawberry scoops on top of
   one another, a spider could be one large scoop beside another small scoop with licorice
   legs.
2. Use the different sizes of ice-cream scoops to scoop out the hard, frozen ice cream from
   the container onto a cold plate.
3. Arrange the scoops of ice cream on the cold plate in the position of the creature's body as
   imagined in step one. Refer to the illustration for ideas.
4. Use the spreading knife to smear and spread the ice cream to smooth the body of the creature, like working with clay.
5. Add appendages and facial features to the cold creature with any selection of other candies
   and fruits. Feel free to discover other foods to decorate the cold creature.
6. Serve as a delicious, delightful dessert.

Good Dog Reward

Ingredients

Serves 2 good dogs

3½ cups all purpose flour, plus extra
1 cup corn meal
½ cup powdered nonfat dry milk
2 cups low-salt chicken stock

1 cup rye flour
2 cups wheat germ
1 package dry yeast
1 beaten egg

Utensils

oven preheated to 300°F
rolling pin
cookie sheet
floured clean surface

large bowl and mixing spoon
cookie cutters (dog bone shape)
pastry brush

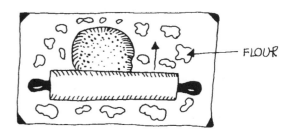
FLOUR

Process

1. Combine all dry ingredients in a bowl. Add chicken stock to the dry ingredients and mix thoroughly.
2. Sprinkle a little flour on the work surface so the dough does not stick.
3. Take a handful of dough and roll it into a ball.
4. Press the ball on the floured clean surface and flatten it to half the thickness. Use the rolling pin to roll the dough.
5. Sprinkle a little flour on top of the dough and turn the dough over. Roll the dough to about ½-inch thick.
6. Cut out the cookies with a cookie cutter.
7. Place the cut-out cookies on the baking sheet and brush the tops of each with the beaten egg.
8. Bake the cookies for 40 minutes.
9. Store in a jar and give to your favorite dog for treats and rewards as deserved, or for no reason at all.

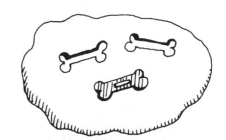

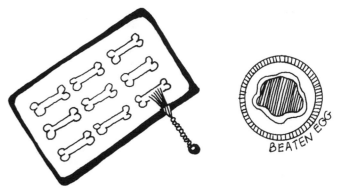
BEATEN EGG

Birthday Pupcake

Serves 2 to 6 dogs

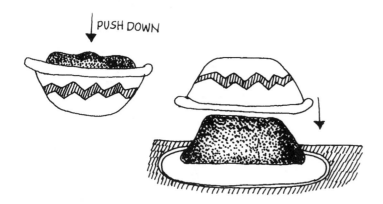

↓ PUSH DOWN

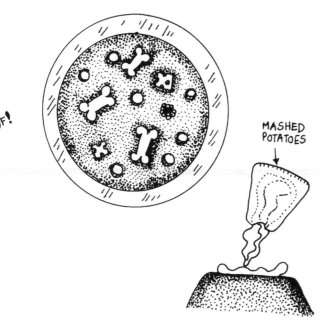

WOOF WOOF!

MASHED POTATOES

Ingredients

2 cans of wet dog (or cat) food   ½ cup of kibbles (dry pet food)
1 box assorted dog (or cat) treats
pet's favorite leftovers for decorations and garnishes, optional, such as
    cheese cubes   sliced hard-boiled eggs
    cooked pasta noodles   meat bits (turkey, chicken, beef)
mashed potatoes in a plastic sandwich bag, optional

WOOF WOOF!

FIDO ♥

Utensils

can opener   measuring cup
mixing bowl and spoon   spreading knife

Process

1. Open the cans of pet food with a can opener and empty them into the mixing bowl.
2. Add the ½ cup of dry pet food to the moist food and mix by hand or with a spoon.
3. Press the pet food into the bottom of the mixing bowl to make a mold.
4. Turn the bowl upside down on a platter and unmold the pet food mixture. When unmolded, the mixture will resemble a cake shape. Smooth any broken edges with the spreading knife.
5. Press pet treats or biscuits into the pet food to decorate the pet cake.
6. If desired, use additional pet food favorites to decorate the cake, such as cheese cubes or bits of meats.
7. For fun — if your pet likes potatoes — cut the corner off the plastic bag filled with mashed potatoes and squeeze a design like icing on the plate or on the cake.
8. Serve your best friend in all the world (the pet) a hearty serving of Birthday Pupcake.
▲ If other animals are invited, serve each one on his own plate, separate from other pet guests. Be sure the pets are good friends and that they are used to sharing without fighting. The authors serve their pet birthday parties outside on the patio or driveway.

Chapter 11

Birds & Bugs

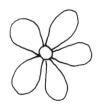

easiest   about 30 minutes   salad

Salad Nests

Serves 2 to 4

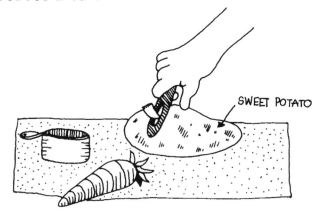

SWEET POTATO

MIX BY HAND

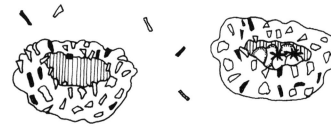

Ingredients

lettuce leaves

1 sweet potato

low-fat vanilla yogurt

foods to resemble "eggs" in the nests, such as
grapes, raisins, cherry tomatoes, hard-boiled eggs

1 to 3 carrots

1 cup chow mein noodles

Utensils

individual salad plates

large bowl

wax paper

vegetable grater

wooden spoon

Process

1. Place a lettuce leaf on each salad plate. Set aside.
2. Scrape off the outer skin of the carrot. Grate enough carrot to make 1 cup. Set aside. Scrape off the outer skin of the sweet potato. Grate enough sweet potato to make 1 cup.
3. Place the grated carrot and sweet potato into a large bowl.
4. Add the chow mein noodles and mix with carrot and sweet potato by hand.
5. Add 1 tablespoon of vanilla yogurt to the noodle mixture and mix until the carrot and sweet potato are well moistened. If more yogurt is needed, add a little at a time.
6. Take a handful of the mixture and shape by hand into several nests.
7. Place one nest on the lettuce on each of the salad plates.
8. Select the eggs for the nest from the remaining ingredients, such as raisins, tomatoes, grapes or hard-boiled eggs, and place them in the nests.
9. Serve immediately to keep noodles crisp.

Caterpillar Cucumber

Ingredients

Serves 4 to 10

shredded lettuce
1 cucumber
any selection of vegetables, such as
    carrot slices, celery slices and leaves, parsley, radishes

Utensils

plate
knife and cutting board
2 wooden spoons
toothpicks

Process

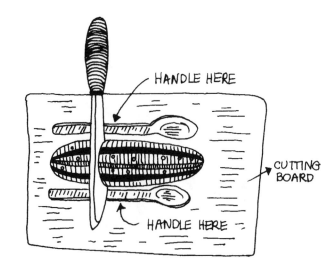

HANDLE HERE

CUTTING BOARD

HANDLE HERE

1. Place the shredded lettuce on the plate. Set aside.
2. Lay the cucumber in the center of the cutting board with the wooden spoon handles placed on each side of the cucumber. The spoons will prevent the cucumber from being sliced all the way through.
3. Cut the cucumber into thin slices, bumping into the spoons with each slice. The thinner the slices, the more sections the cucumber caterpillar will have.
4. Attach the remaining ingredients with toothpicks to the caterpillar to make facial features or spots. Vegetables can be placed between slices too. Any caterpillar design is delicious.
5. Arrange the caterpillar on the shredded lettuce to serve as a salad snack.
▲ Remove the toothpicks before eating.

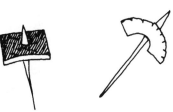

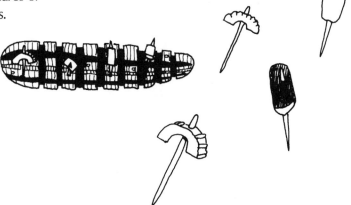

easier

about 30 minutes

bake

breakfast

Fluffy Breakfast Nest

Serves 1 or 2

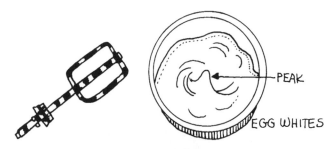
PEAK
EGG WHITES

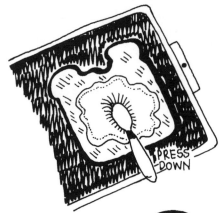
PRESS DOWN

Ingredients

2 slices bread
2 eggs

butter
salt and pepper

Utensils

oven preheated to 350°F
butter knife
2 bowls
spoon

oven mitt
baking sheet
electric mixer
spatula

Process

1. Place two slices of bread in a toaster and toast very lightly.
2. Spread butter on the toast with a butter knife. Place the buttered toast on the baking sheet. Set aside.
3. Crack each egg and let the whites fall into a bowl. Then, put the yolks fall into a separate bowl. Be careful not to break the yolks.
4. Beat the egg whites with the electric mixer until they form stiff pointed peaks.
5. Spoon egg whites onto each slice of toast. Take the spoon and form a dent in the center of the egg white mound to make nest pockets.
6. Carefully spoon one egg yolk into each egg white dent.
7. Place the baking sheet with toast and eggs in the oven and bake until the whites turn brown and the yolks are cooked through, usually about 4 minutes
8. Wear an oven mitt and remove the baking sheet from the oven.
9. Place the nests on a plate with a spoon or spatula to serve.

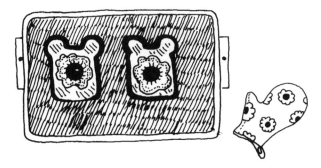

Cooking Art

Hoagie the Hot Caterpillar

sandwich   bake   about 45 minutes   easiest

Ingredients

Serves 4 to 8

¼ cup mayonnaise
2 teaspoons prepared mustard
1 loaf Italian bread
10 to 12 slices cheese

3 teaspoons parsley
½ teaspoon onion powder
10 to 12 slices luncheon meat
shredded lettuce

Utensils

oven preheated to 375°F
cutting board
bread knife

small mixing bowl and spoon
2 wooden spoons
aluminum foil

Process

1. Place the mayonnaise, parsley, mustard and onion powder in a bowl and mix with the spoon. Set aside.
2. Place the bread on a cutting board. Place two wooden spoon handles alongside the bread on the cutting board as a guide to prevent cutting all the way through the bread.
3. Cut the bread into 10 equal slices with a knife, cutting only until knife touches the wooden spoon handles. The bread will resemble a caterpillar with sections.
4. Spread the mayonnaise mixture on every other slice of bread.
5. Fold the luncheon meat and cheese in halves or thirds and tuck a slice of folded meat and cheese into every slot with the mayonnaise mixture in it. Do not place anything in the folds without mayonnaise.
6. Wrap the loaf in aluminum foil. Put the wrapped sandwich in the oven and bake for 25 minutes. Wear an oven mitt and remove the sandwich from the oven. Set aside briefly.
7. Sprinkle a thick layer of shredded lettuce on the plate
8. Place the caterpillar hoagie sandwich on the lettuce "grass" to serve.
9. When ready to eat the hoagie caterpillar, cut or tear in the spaces that are empty and were not filled with sandwich makings.

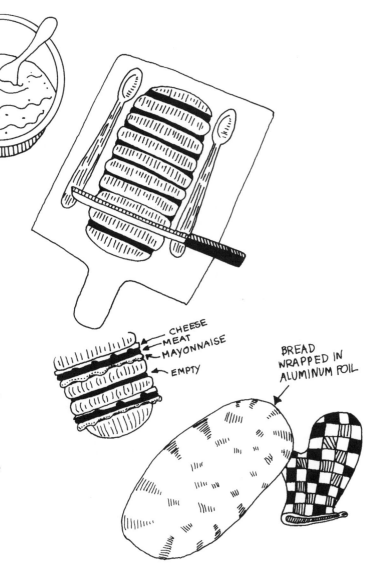

CHEESE
MEAT
MAYONNAISE
EMPTY

BREAD WRAPPED IN ALUMINUM FOIL

Birds & Bugs

Spider Sandwiches

Serves 6 to 10

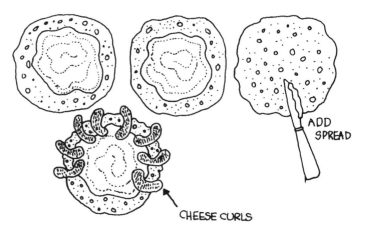

ADD SPREAD

CHEESE CURLS

Ingredients

24 slices wheat sandwich bread
1½ cups of any sandwich spread, such as
   peanut butter, tuna salad, soft cheese
1 can cheese curls or pretzel sticks
24 raisins

Utensils

cookie cutter, 2½ inch round
plain paper plates
black permanent marker

Process

1. Place the bread slices on the work surface. Cut a circle from each bread slice with the cookie cutter.
2. Divide the bread circles into two equal piles.
3. Spread about 2 tablespoons of sandwich spread on all of the bread circles in one pile.
4. Press eight cheese curls or pretzel sticks in the sandwich spread half way around each circle to make the legs of the spider.
5. Place the remaining bread circle on top of the sandwich spread coated circles.
6. Using a finger, poke 2 small indentations on top of each sandwich. Push 1 raisin into each indentation to make the eyes.
7. Draw a spider web with the permanent black marker on a paper plate. Place one spider on each plate and serve for a silly lunch.

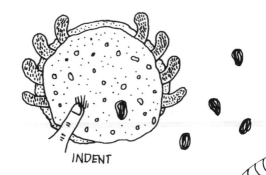

INDENT

Flutterby Sandwiches

Ingredients

1 large package cream cheese
2 slices white bread per person
food coloring or fruit juice
choices or variety of small food items, such as

olives	dried fruit bits	raisins
celery bits	carrot sticks	mushroom slices

romaine lettuce leaf per person

Utensils

knife and cutting board
small bowls, one for each color
small spoons, one for each color
butter knives, one for each color

Process

1. Cut the cream cheese block into 3 or 4 equal parts with a knife.
2. Place each section of cream cheese in a small bowl. Add 1 drop of food coloring to each bowl. Each bowl will have a different color.
3. Mix the food coloring (or juice) and cream cheese with a spoon until well blended. Use a different spoon for each color. Set aside.
4. Cut the bread in half diagonally with a knife to create two butterfly wings.
5. Place the two points of the butterfly wings together on the plate. The two points will have crust on the corners. The crustless part of the bread will face out. See the illustration.
6. Spread the colored cream cheese on the wings with butter knives to make colors and patterns.
7. Add additional decoration with food pieces to create antennae and any other butterfly features, real or imagined.
8. Place a romaine lettuce leaf on the plate to give the butterfly a place to show off its wings. Place the butterfly on the leaf. Serve as a snack or lunch.

Allow 1 butterfly per person

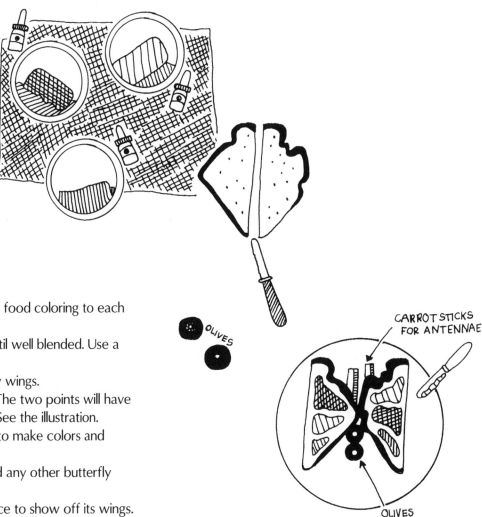

OLIVES

CARROT STICKS FOR ANTENNAE

OLIVES

Veggie Bird Modeling

Serves 1 or more

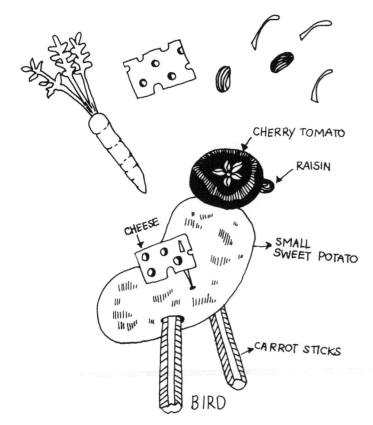

CHERRY TOMATO

RAISIN

CHEESE

SMALL SWEET POTATO

CARROT STICKS

BIRD

Ingredients

choose any of the following foods

cheese slices	raisins	bean sprouts
cherry tomatoes	cucumber slices	alfalfa sprouts
pearl onions	carrot sticks	other foods of choice

Utensils

kitchen scissors
knife and cutting board
toothpicks
plate

Process

1. Study the foods available and imagine the types of birds or animals that can be designed, created or sculpted using the foods. (For example, carrot sticks for legs, cherry tomato for a head.) See the illustration.
2. Construct a bird by arranging the foods on the plate. Use toothpicks to connect parts, if needed. Use kitchen scissors and a knife to make shapes and different sizes.
3. After the bird design has been created, serve as a light snack or salad. Add a favorite vegetable dip, if desired.
▲ Remember to remove toothpicks before eating.

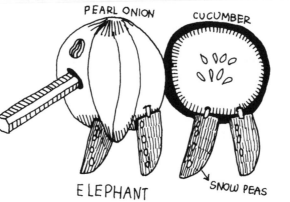

PEARL ONION   CUCUMBER

ELEPHANT

SNOW PEAS

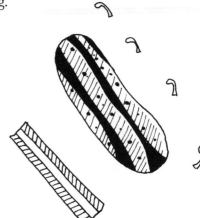

Nest in a Basket

Ingredients

Serves 6

3 large shredded wheat biscuits
1½ tablespoons light brown sugar
1½ cups low-fat vanilla yogurt
lettuce leaves or sprouts, optional

⅓ cup shredded coconut
⅓ cup butter or margarine, melted
1 cup grapes

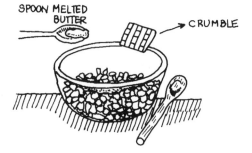

SPOON MELTED BUTTER

CRUMBLE

Utensils

oven preheated to 350°F
aluminum foil
medium mixing bowl and spoon

muffin tins
3 to 6 serving plates
oven mitt

Process

1. Line the muffin cups with aluminum foil, letting some foil overhang each cup. Set aside.
2. Place a lettuce leaf or large pinch of sprouts on each salad plate. Set aside.
3. Crumble the shredded wheat into the mixing bowl. Add the coconut and brown sugar to the crumbled shredded wheat and mix together with the mixing spoon.
4. Pour the melted butter over the shredded wheat mixture and mix well.
5. Press the shredded wheat mixture onto the bottom and up the sides of the muffin cups.
6. Place the muffin tin in the oven and bake for 10 minutes, or until wheat biscuit mixture is light golden brown and crisp. Wear an oven mitt and remove the muffin tin from the oven. Cool for 30 minutes.
7. Remove the nests from the pans by lifting the foil by the edges. Gently peel the foil off the nest baskets.
8. Place the nest basket on a salad plate covered with lettuce or sprouts.
9. Place 2 to 3 tablespoons of yogurt in the bottom of each nest basket. Place grapes in the nest baskets on top of the yogurt to resemble eggs.

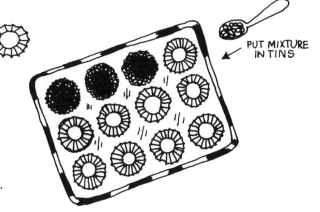

PUT MIXTURE IN TINS

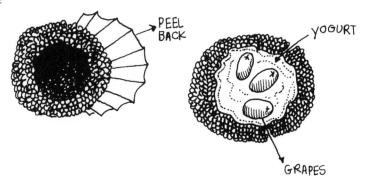

PEEL BACK

YOGURT

GRAPES

Sweet Spider Web

Serves 1 as described — recipe can be doubled, tripled or made quite large for lots of small spiders or several very large spiders

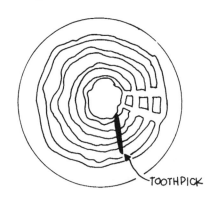

TOOTHPICK

COCOA

PEANUT BUTTER + SUGAR

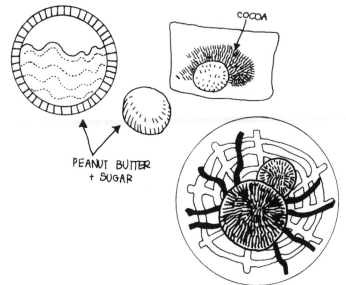

Ingredients

1 cup chocolate syrup in squeeze bottle, such as Hersheys
1 tablespoon cocoa
1 tablespoon powdered sugar

1 tablespoon peanut butter
8 chow mein noodles or licorice laces

Utensils

small plate
small dish

toothpick
mixing bowl

Process

1. Squeeze a small circle in the center of the plate with the chocolate sauce.
2. Draw another circle around the first one leaving at least ¼ inch between the circles. Draw several more circles around the first two. Always leave at least ¼ inch between each circle.
3. To make the circles into a web, place a toothpick in the center of the first (smallest) chocolate circle. Drag the toothpick through the second and all remaining circles, toward the outside edge of the plate. This makes the first spoke of the spider web.
4. Continue making several more spokes until the circles look like a completed web. Set aside.
5. Sprinkle cocoa in a small dish. Set aside.
6. Mix the peanut butter and the powdered sugar together in the bowl. Knead and mix the peanut butter and sugar together with hands, forming two balls, a large one for the spider's body and a small one for its head.
7. Gently roll the balls in the cocoa to make the spider's body look fuzzy.
8. Stick 8 chow mien noodles or licorice laces into the spider body to create legs.
9. Place the spider on the spider web and serve for a sweet dessert.

Apple Puff Bugs

Ingredients

Serves 4 to 8

about 20 raisins
1 tablespoon milk
vanilla yogurt

½ cup orange juice
refrigerated crescent roll dough
food coloring, optional

1 egg yolk
4 medium apples
lettuce leaf

Utensils

oven preheated to 400°F
3 cups for mixing
fork
melon scoop
pastry brush
oven mitt

measuring cups and spoons
scissors or knife
baking sheet
knife and cutting board
spoon for yogurt

Process

1. Soak all the raisins in the cup orange juice for several hours or overnight in the refrigerator.
2. Mix one egg yolk and 1 tablespoon of milk in a cup. Set aside.
3. Open the crescent roll dough and separate it into squares. With the scissors or knife, trim the corners off the squares, shaping the squares into circles for bugs' bodies. Cut the dough in shapes of bugs with legs and appendages or other creatures like frogs, toads, rabbits, dinosaurs or monsters. Prick the shapes with the fork and place them on the baking sheet. Set aside.
4. Cut the apples in half. Scrape out the seeds and core with the melon scoop. Leave the skins on. Then, slice the apples into ½-inch thick circles.
5. Brush the puff bug shapes with a little egg yolk and milk to glaze the dough. Place a round apple slice on each puff bug. Smaller pieces of apple can be used in any way too, even for nibbling while cooking. Add the orange-soaked raisins for eyes or other bug features and decorations.
6. Bake the Apple Puff Bugs for 15 to 20 minutes or until the dough is golden and puffy and the apples are soft. When they are done, wear an oven mitt and remove the Apple Puff Bugs from the oven. Cool on the baking sheet.
7. Meanwhile, mix a drop or two of food coloring with the vanilla yogurt, or leave it plain. Place a lettuce leaf on a serving plate. Spoon a puddle of yogurt on the leaf. Place a hot Puff Bug in the yogurt and serve as a warm dessert.

▲ Other fruits may be substituted for the apple, such as, peaches, bananas or pears.

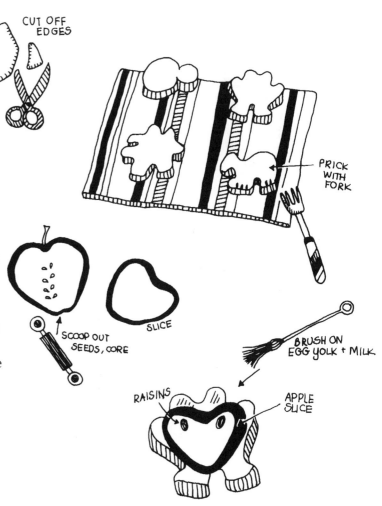

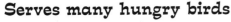
Bird Berries

Serves many hungry birds

Ingredients

package of fresh cranberries

Utensils

embroidery floss, dental floss or thin, strong string
large plastic needle

Process

1. Thread the string through the eye of the needle.
2. Pull one end of the string almost all the way through. Then, tie a double knot at the end of the string.
3. Next, lace or string the needle through the cranberries forming a garland, like beads on a necklace.
4. When the string is full, clip the string from the needle and tie another knot to hold.
5. Make additional cranberry strings to attach to the first, or stop with one string. If additional strings are made, tie each one to the one before to make an extra long string of cranberries.
6. When ready, drape the cranberry string over the branches of a tree outside for the birds to discover and enjoy for food.
7. When the birds have finished the berries, remove the string and discard.

▲ Other foods may be added to the string, such as dry round cereal, pieces of stale bread or bagels, dried carrot slices and so on. Take a look in the cupboard and see what can be found that birds enjoy.

BREAD

CARROT

CEREAL

BAGEL

Chapter 12

A Year Full of Special Days

Celebration Cakes

Any Time

ICING
CANDY

FIRST DAY OF SPRING!

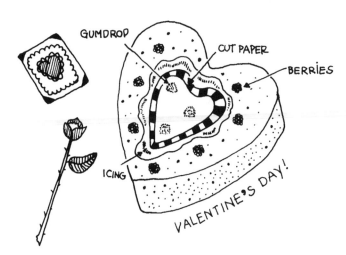

GUMDROP
CUT PAPER
BERRIES
ICING
VALENTINE'S DAY!

Ingredients

any cake, any flavor, any shape
decoration frosting (see recipes on page 145)
choice of favorite decorations, such as

sprinkles	fruit	gumdrops
candy	flowers	nuts
candles	paper cutouts	

Utensils

selection of decorating tools, such as

pastry bag	plastic bag	decorating tube
spreader	string	knife
toothpick	fingers	

something to serve and display the cake on, such as

serving platter	tray	cake plate
lined basket	cake pan	covered cardboard gift box
fabric-covered board		

Process

1. One of the most creative, most appreciated recipes a cook can prepare is a special cake for a special day. Look at the illustrations for ideas of celebration cake shapes and decorations. Basic cakes can be cut or assembled into new shapes. Cake pans can be purchased in such shapes as Easter eggs, hearts and funny cowboys.

2. Create your own new and unusual cake ideas! Imagination is the key. Suggestions of days to celebrate and appreciate with a fancy cake include:

birthdays	first day of spring	first tooth out
holidays of all kinds	first day of school	first snowfall
new baby	unbirthdays	home from the hospital
tied shoes	grandma's visit	just 'cause

3. Celebrate "Theme Days," such as

clown day	under the sea	letters and numbers
I Love You	seasons	special friends
recycling	the sky	colors
shapes	big and little	rainy day
pets	insects	collection day
peanut day	pickle day	play and fun day

Basic Frosting Recipes for the Best Decorating Frostings Ever

Buttercream Piping Icing — for piping flowers, lines, stars and other shapes from a pastry bag or decorating tube.

1. Blend 2 boxes sifted confectioners' sugar with 2 cups (4 sticks) butter and a sprinkle of salt.

2. Add about 2 teaspoons of lemon, orange or vanilla extract, and 4 to 8 tablespoons of milk.

3. Blend all these together, adding food coloring drops or paste, if desired. Icing should be smooth, but not too thin. Variations of flavors:

✔ **Orange**: Use orange juice instead of milk.

✔ **Nutmeg or Cinnamon**: Add 1 to 2 teaspoons of nutmeg or cinnamon to the basic recipe. Add a little molasses and a little less milk, if desired.

✔ **Peppermint**: Use peppermint extract instead of others. Add some finely crushed peppermint candies to the powdered sugar.

✔ **Chocolate**: Add ¼ cup unsweetened cocoa to the powdered sugar.

✔ **Mocha**: Add ¼ cup unsweetened cocoa and 2 teaspoons instant coffee granules to the butter.

✔ **Maple**: Use ¼ cup maple syrup in place of the milk. A little extra sugar may be needed.

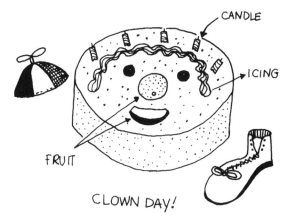

CANDLE

ICING

FRUIT

CLOWN DAY!

BAG PART

PASTRY BAG

Hard Glue Icing — especially good for a smooth, hard finish, or for building and architectural uses, such as gingerbread houses and cakes or cookies where a strong, glue-type icing is needed.

1. Mix 6 egg whites, 1 teaspoon cream of tartar and 2 boxes sifted powdered sugar (confectioners' sugar) with an electric mixer on low speed for several minutes.
2. Beat on high for 4 to 10 minutes until icing forms stiff peaks. Do not over beat this icing or it will become dry and hard to use. Keep Hard Glue Icing covered with a damp towel or snap-on lid when not in use or while waiting to use.
3. Add food coloring or food pastes. Can be frozen.

▲ Use squeaky clean bowls and utensils when making this icing, because oils or grease will keep it from working effectively.

▲ Add about 1 teaspoon lemon, orange or vanilla extract for flavoring. Meringue powder works perfectly when substituted for confectioners' sugar.

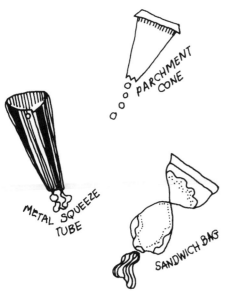

PARCHMENT CONE

METAL SQUEEZE TUBE

SANDWICH BAG

Smooth Cover Icing — for smooth, shiny glaze coverings on cakes and cookies and for filling in outlines made with Buttercream or Hard Glue Icings.

Thin the Hard Glue Icing recipe with a little water, but do not make the icing too thin. To be sure of the proper consistency, drizzle a little icing on the cookie or cake and see if the icing flows or blends slowly. If it blends quickly or immediately, it is too thin. Add little pinches of sifted confectioners' sugar to thicken. Keep covered like Hard Glue Icing.

Decorating Bags

Pastry Bag — fabric bag with choices of tips, joined to the bag with a coupler.

Parchment Cone — disposable paper tube formed from a parchment triangle with the end snipped off.

Metal Squeeze Tube — inexpensive metal tube with a plunger to force icing out. Works well, but not as artistic as the pastry bag.

Sandwich Bag — fill a sandwich bag with frosting. Twist the bag so the frosting is forced towards one corner. Snip the corner making a small or large hole, and squeeze the frosting out through the corner like a pastry bag.

Basic Icing Dough

dessert

about 30 minutes

easier

Any Time

Ingredients

5 cups powdered sugar
2 egg whites
6 tablespoons corn syrup
butter
paste food coloring, thinned with a few drops of water, in cups

Utensils

measuring cups and spoons
plastic wrap
rolling pin
fine point paintbrushes, clean
serving tray lined with foil or wax paper

mixing bowl and spoon
buttered wooden board
butter knife or cookie cutters
cupcakes or cookies, optional

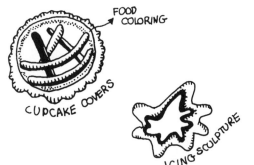

Process

Icing Dough

Icing Dough is useful in decorating cakes, cookies and other desserts with personalized creative sculptures and designs.

1. Measure four cups of powdered sugar in a bowl. Add two egg whites and 6 tablespoons corn syrup. Mix and stir, gradually adding another cup of powdered sugar. Mixture will form a stiff dough. Refrigerate in plastic wrap if not being used immediately.
2. Knead the dough until pliable and soft. Use to decorate cookies, cakes or other desserts. See ideas in box to the right.

Rolled Icing Dough Shapes

1. Place the icing dough on the buttered board. Flatten the dough by hand or roll it out with a rolling pin.
2. Cut shapes from the dough with a butter knife or cookie cutters.
3. Paint designs on the dough shapes with food coloring and a clean brush.
4. Place on a serving tray lined with foil or waxed paper. Refrigerate until coloring is dry. Use as decorations for cakes or garnish for fancy desserts.

Cupcake Covers

1. Roll out the icing dough and cut a circle the size of a cupcake top.
2. Paint a design with food coloring on the circle.
3. Place on the cupcake. Refrigerate until coloring design is dry.
▲ Decorate round cookies with the same technique.

Icing Sculpture

1. Roll icing dough into balls or shapes. Sculpt animals, flowers or designs.
2. Dip a finger in water to smooth cracks or to stick pieces of dough together.
3. Paint with food coloring. Refrigerate until dry.

easier   about 30 minutes   bake   dessert

Any Time

Basic Kid-Size Gingerbread Recipe

Ingredients

1 stick butter or margarine
1 teaspoon salt
4 tablespoons water
cooking oil
6 to 8 teaspoons pumpkin pie spice
¾ cup light or dark molasses

1 cup white or brown sugar
1 teaspoon baking soda
4 cups flour, plus extra

▲ If you don't have pumpkin pie spice, use a mixture of cloves, nutmeg and cinnamon.
▲ For light-colored gingerbread dough, use honey instead of the molasses.

Utensils

oven preheated to 350°F
large bowl and wooden spoon
rolling pin

measuring cups and spoons
plastic wrap
cookie sheet

Process

This recipe can be used for small houses, cottages, other small gingerbread sculptures or for cookies.

1. Mix 1 stick butter or margarine and 1 cup white or brown sugar in a large bowl.
2. Blend in the salt, baking soda and pumpkin pie spice.
3. Stir in the molasses and water. Add the flour. Mix well.
4. Form a ball of dough by working the ingredients together by hand.
5. Wrap the dough in plastic. Chill the dough for several hours.
6. Roll out the dough to ¼-inch thick. Form walls for houses, shapes or cookies.
7. Bake on lightly oiled cookie sheets for 8 to 20 minutes, depending on the size of the pieces.
8. Cool.
9. Use the icings listed on pages 145-7 to build a cottage or decorate cookies.

Frosty Fruit Snowflakes

bake　　dessert　　about 30 minutes　　easiest

Ingredients

small flour tortillas, one per person
white sugar
butter
confectioners' sugar
grapes, raspberries and peeled orange sections

Utensils

kitchen scissors　　　　　　　　　　baking sheet
pastry brush or spreading knife　　　small bowl

Process

1. Fold the tortilla in half, then fold in half again.
2. With kitchen scissors, cut shapes and holes on the folds of the tortilla, similar to cutting a snowflake from paper, cutting through all layers of the tortilla. Remove the cut-away pieces to nibble while working. Unfold and open the tortilla snowflake.
3. Place the tortilla snowflake on the baking sheet. Create as many snowflake tortillas as desired. Place all of them on the baking sheet.
4. Brush each snowflake with a little butter. Sprinkle with a little white sugar.
5. Place the snowflakes under the oven broiler to brown and crisp just a little, usually about 2 to 5 minutes.
6. Put the confectioners' sugar in a small bowl. Set aside.
7. Wash the raspberries and grapes. Peel and section the orange.
8. Dip the wet fruits — grapes, raspberries and orange sections — in the confectioners' sugar and arrange them on the broiled snowflake tortillas.
9. Serve as a light and bright sweetened fruit snack on a dark, wintry afternoon.

January

Allow 1 fruit tortilla per person

TORTILLA

→ SUGAR

→ BUTTER

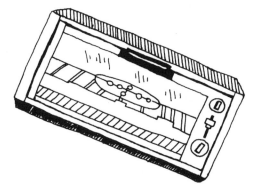

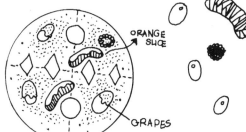

SUGAR

ORANGE SLICE

GRAPES

Jack Frost Treat

January

Makes about 6 snowflakes

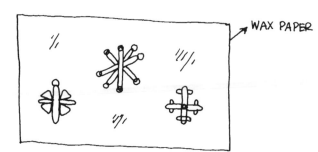

Ingredients

4 cups confectioners' sugar
3 tablespoons meringue powder (available at kitchen supply stores)
6 tablespoons warm water
edible glitter or decorative sugar sprinkles

Utensils

baking sheet	wax paper
large bowl	electric mixer
pastry bag with number 10 point	paintbrush
spatula	nylon thread

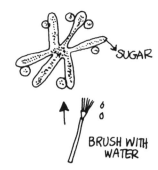

Process

1. Cover the baking sheet with wax paper. Set aside.
2. Place the confectioners' sugar, meringue powder and water in the large bowl. Beat the sugar mixture on low speed with the electric mixer until well mixed. Turn the electric mixer up to high and beat the mixture for up to 7 minutes or until stiff peaks form.
3. Spoon the sugary meringue into the pastry bag.
4. Make snowflake designs, each about the size of a walnut, on the wax paper-covered baking sheet. Draw a line first, then make lines over top of the first one. Add curls, circles, triangles and different shapes that resemble a snowflake.
5. Dip the paintbrush in water and very lightly paint water over each snowflake. Sprinkle the glitter or sugar sprinkles over the snowflakes before the water dries.
6. Let the snowflakes dry.
7. Carefully remove the snowflakes from the wax paper with a spatula.
8. Very carefully, tie a thread to each snowflake and hang, if desired. Snowflakes (or any other shape) may also be used to garnish or decorate cakes, cupcakes or other wintry recipes, and they are delicious to eat at any time.

Washington's Cherry Tree Pillows

February

Serves 4

Ingredients

1 sheet frozen puff pastry, such as Pepperidge Farm Frozen Puff Pastry
1 can cherry pie filling
confectioners' sugar

Utensils

oven preheated to 425°F
measuring cups
oven mitt
markers or fabric pens, optional

knife
baking sheet
spatula
heavy paper napkins, optional

Process

1. Open the puff pastry package and thaw on the countertop for about 15 minutes.
2. Cut a long strip of dough about ¼-inch wide all the way down one side. Set aside.
3. Cut the remaining pastry sheet into four 4-inch squares. In the center of each square, place about ⅛ cup of cherry pie filling.
4. Bring pastry corners together just above cherry pie filling, twist the top and turn to hold in place, like a pillow or bundle. Place the pillow on the baking sheet.
5. Next, cut off a section of the strip of dough and make a bow on the pillow. Pinch the bow into the top of the pillow pastry.
6. Bake the cherry pillows in the oven for 10 to 15 minutes until golden brown. Wear an oven mitt and remove the hot cherry pillows from the oven. Cool for 10 minutes.
7. Sprinkle the tops of the pillows with soft, powdery confectioners' sugar.
8. For additional creative fun, draw on white paper napkins with permanent markers to create plate liners that look like quilts, or color fabric squares with fabric pens for the same results.
9. Place a quilt napkin on each plate. Transfer the cherry pillows to quilted serving plates.

▲ Serve as a dessert even George Washington would love. I cannot tell a lie! Cherry Tree Pillows are delicious.

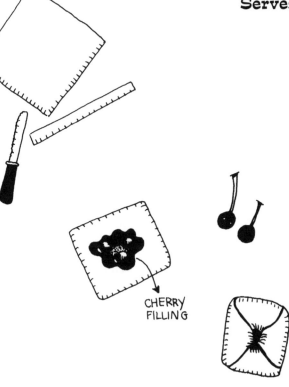

CHERRY FILLING

BOW

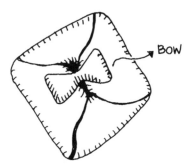

Valentine Wigglers

February

Serves 2 to 4

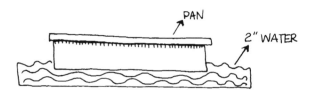

PAN
2" WATER

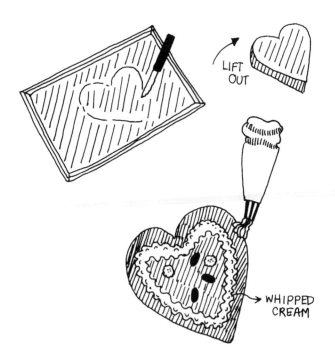

LIFT OUT

WHIPPED CREAM

Ingredients

4 small packages red gelatin, such as Jell-O
2½ cups boiling water
whipped topping, thawed
bits of fresh fruits or nuts for garnish, such as

| apple | strawberry | banana |
| raspberries | almonds | ground walnuts |

Utensils

large glass measuring cup-mixing bowl
rubber spatula or scraper for stirring
plastic knife
pastry bag

measuring cup
rectangular pan
spoon

Process

1. Pour the four boxes of red gelatin into a large glass measuring cup-mixing bowl that has a handle and pouring spout.
2. Add the boiling water to the gelatin and stir the mixture slowly with the rubber spatula until the gelatin completely dissolves. Scrape the sides of the bowl while stirring so all the granules are dissolved. Pour the gelatin into the rectangular pan. (Don't be surprised if there are spills.)
3. Place the pan of gelatin in the refrigerator and let it chill until it is firm, usually for several hours. When chilled and firm, remove the pan from the refrigerator.
4. To loosen the gelatin from the pan, dip the bottom of pan in a sink filled with 2 inches of warm water for a few seconds. Set the pan of gelatin on the work surface again.
5. Trace a large heart shape or pattern in the gelatin. Cut the line with a knife.
6. Carefully—and with two or more hands—lift the heart out of pan and place it on a serving plate.
7. Next, spoon some thick whipped topping into the pastry bag. Squeeze the bag gently to make designs or to write on the gelatin heart. Decorate around the heart too, if desired. Garnish with bits of fresh fruits or nuts.
8. The leftover gelatin can be cut with small cookie cutters or cut into cubes with a knife to further decorate the heart dessert. Or, the leftovers can be nibbled now or enjoyed later.

Shamrock Rolls

Ingredients

nonstick cooking spray
butter, softened

frozen bread dough in small rolls
green food coloring

Utensils

oven preheated to 350°F
baking sheet
melon ball scoop
small dish for butter balls
spatula

knife
bowl and spoon
bowl of ice water
oven mitt

March

Serves 5 to 10

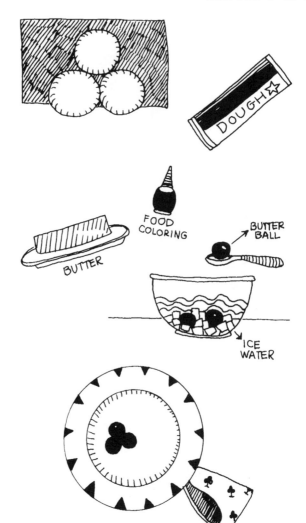

Process

1. Spray a light coating of cooking spray on the baking sheet.
2. Open the package of dough and let it thaw.
3. Cut each roll of dough into 3 pieces (or 4 for lucky four-leaf clovers). Shape each dough piece by hand into a ball.
4. Place the balls together in a triangular formation on the baking sheet and push them close together. See the illustration. This will make a clover or shamrock-shaped roll when baked. Make as many rolls as the package will allow, usually about 5 to 10.
5. Bake the shamrock-shaped rolls just until they are golden brown, usually about 4 to 8 minutes.
6. While the rolls are baking, mix a stick of slightly softened butter with a few drops of green food coloring. Scoop balls of green butter and drop the balls into a bowl of ice water to chill and harden.
7. Place 3 or 4 chilled butter balls on a small plate in the shape of a shamrock or clover.
8. Wear an oven mitt and take the rolls out of the oven. Transfer them with a spatula to a serving plate.
9. Serve the shamrock rolls with shamrock butter balls for a delightful green treat any leprechaun would love.

Sandwich Kites

March

Serves 2 to 4

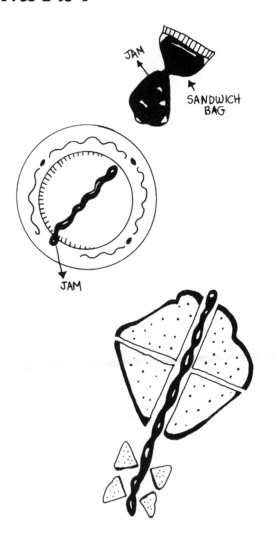

JAM

SANDWICH
BAG

JAM

Ingredients

8 slices of square white bread
peanut butter
choice of jelly or jam for decoration

Utensils

knife and cutting board
spoon
scissors

spreading knife
plastic sandwich bag
large plate

PEANUT
BUTTER

Process

1. Cut the crusts from the 8 slices of white bread. Place the bread slices on a work surface.
2. Spread peanut butter on 4 slices of bread. Place the plain bread on top of the peanut butter to make a sandwich.
3. Cut the bread in half from corner to corner to make 2 triangles per sandwich. Set aside.
4. Choose jelly or jam for the decoration. Fill a plastic sandwich bag with a little jelly-a few tablespoons should do. Cut the point off the corner of the bag. Hold the bag tightly shut by twisting the rest of the bag. Squeeze a wiggly line of fruit jam from the corner of the bag, making a design down the center of the plate. See the illustration.
5. Place one triangle on each side of the line, at the top of the line, to create a kite body.
6. Cut the remaining triangles in half again, starting at the points. This will make 4 small triangles. To make the kite tail, place the small triangles alongside the line with the points facing one another. See the illustration.
7. The kite is ready for serving as a spring lunch.
▲ Kite Sandwiches can be made with any sandwich filling and square shaped bread slices.

Fancy Egg Bread

bread   bake   1 hour or more   easier

Ingredients

1 loaf frozen bread dough
2 raw decorated eggs (see page 156 for decorating ideas)
1 raw egg
1 tablespoon milk

Utensils

oven preheated to 350°F   bread pan
knife and cutting board   small bowls
whisk or fork   pastry brush
oven mitt

Process

1. Place the frozen bread dough in a bread pan to thaw.
2. Cut two slits in the thawed dough with a knife. The slits should be the size of eggs.
3. Put one decorated egg in each slit of the dough. Allow at least half of the egg to show. Set aside.
4. Crack open the plain raw egg and separate, keeping the yolk in a separate bowl.
5. Mix the egg yolk and milk together.
6. Brush the top of the bread with the egg yolk and milk mixture.
7. Place the bread in the oven and bake according to bread dough package directions (usually about 30 minutes at 350°F), until it is a rich brown color and hollow sounding when tapped with a knife handle. Wear an oven mitt and remove the baked bread from the oven.
8. Serve in a basket lined with a pastel napkin or cloth. Bread is served by each person tearing away a serving of bread by hand. The two eggs will be baked through and solid and may be eaten like hard-boiled eggs.

April

Serves 4 to 8

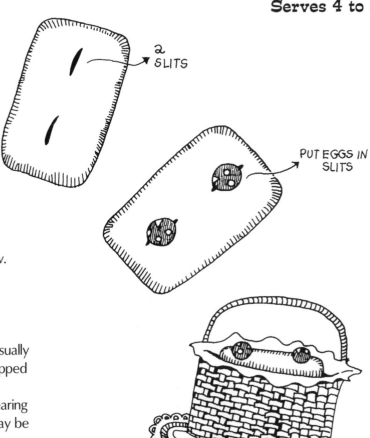

2 SLITS

PUT EGGS IN SLITS

easier   about 30 minutes   snack

Easy Stenciled Eggs

April

Allow 1 or 2 eggs per person

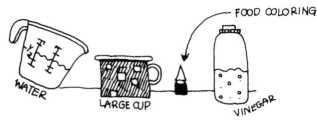

WATER   LARGE CUP   FOOD COLORING   VINEGAR

Ingredients
food coloring
½ cup boiling water for each color of food coloring to make the egg dye
vinegar
hard-boiled eggs, cooled and completely dry

Utensils

measuring cup	1 large cup for each egg dye color
scissors	1 soup spoon for each egg dye color
masking tape	stick-on polka dots (from craft stores)
tablespoon	paper towels

Easter grass, optional basket, optional

Process

1. Place a few drops of food coloring in each cup.
2. Pour ½ cup boiling water into each cup with the food coloring. Add 1 tablespoon of vinegar to each cup of colored water. Stir with the spoons to mix well. This is the egg dye. Set the cups of dye aside.
3. Using the scissors, cut the masking tape into strips, letters and shapes. Stick the masking tape shapes on the eggs and rub with a fingernail or the back of a spoon to make the tape stick to the egg. Add the stick-on dots, too, if desired, rubbing these in the same way to stick.
4. Next, carefully lower the egg into a cup of food coloring using a soup spoon.
5. Gently move, roll and dip the egg thoroughly in the egg dye with a spoon so the dye is spread evenly over the egg.
6. When the color is as dark as desired, lift the egg out of the dye. Dry the egg gently with a paper towel. Remove the masking tape and dots from the egg. If desired, place the egg in a different cup of dye, repeating the process of thoroughly covering the egg with color. Continue dyeing the eggs until all are bright and colorful.
7. Place some Easter grass in a basket and place the eggs on the grass as a decoration. Then, use the same basket of eggs to serve the hard-boiled eggs as a snack, cold breakfast with toast or to make deviled eggs.

In the Pink for Mom

breakfast

about 30 minutes

easy

Ingredients

strawberries and 1 banana
vanilla or strawberry yogurt
English muffin
powdered sugar

cream cheese in a small bowl or cup
cranberry juice
tea bag and sugar cubes

May

Serves 1 very special mom

Utensils

For the tray
  pink or white napkin, place mat or fabric rectangle
  pink ribbons, flowers or blossoms   hole punch and paper, optional
  vase or saucer
For the food
  knife and cutting board   small mixing bowls and spoons
  spreading knife   juice glass
  tea cup and small tea pot

Process

Prepare the tray

1. Cover the tray with a pretty pink or white napkin, fabric or place mat.
2. Decorate the tray with little ribbons, flowers and/or streamers. Sprinkle confetti made with a paper punch around the tray. Place a flower in a vase or float a blossom on a saucer and place on the tray.

Prepare the breakfast

1. Put the cream cheese in a small bowl.
2. Chop up a few strawberries with a knife. Stir them into the cream cheese. Set aside.
3. Slice the remaining strawberries and the banana and put them in a small serving bowl or custard cup. Put a dollop of yogurt on top of the strawberries and bananas. Set aside.
4. Pour cranberry juice in a juice glass and set on the tray.
5. Pour boiling water into the small tea pot. Set on the tray with the tea cup and the tea bag.
6. Toast the English muffin. When warm and brown, spread the cream cheese-strawberry mixture on the muffin.
7. Assemble everything on the tray and carry it to Mom's bed for a Mother's Day surprise breakfast in bed that's "in the pink".

▲ Substitute any pink or white foods or decorations that this very special mom might enjoy.

Flower Fruit Bread

May

Serves 1

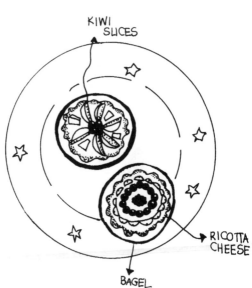

KIWI SLICES

RICOTTA CHEESE

BAGEL

Ingredients

favorite bread, such as
   English muffin, banana bread, biscuit or bagel, sandwich bread
ricotta cheese or cottage cheese
fresh fruits, such as
   kiwi
   grapes
   strawberries
   peaches
   raspberries
   blueberries

Utensils

spreading knife
knife and cutting board

Process

1. Spread any favorite bread with the ricotta or cottage cheese.
2. Slice the fruits into small pieces.
3. Decorate the bread with the fruits to make flower burst designs or other designs. See illustration.
4. Eat and enjoy this simple, delicious snack or light breakfast.

Father's Famous Favorite Family Toast

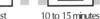
June

Serves 1 or more

Ingredients

4 colors of food coloring
6 slices white bread
¼ cup milk

Utensils

4 custard cups
4 spoons
paintbrush

FOOD COLORING

Process

1. Place several drops of different colored food coloring in each custard cup.
2. Add equal amounts of milk to the food coloring and mix well with a spoon, using a separate spoon for each cup.
3. Place the bread in the toaster and toast just until the bread hardens. Do not let it turn brown.
4. Paint the faces or initials of each family member on the toast pieces with a paintbrush dipped in the milky food coloring.
5. Arrange the toast paintings on the serving platter for a Father's Breakfast Surprise.
6. Serve with other breakfast foods of choice, such as scrambled eggs, sliced oranges or grilled ham.
7. Add some of Dad's favorite breakfast items, like coffee or juice, to complete the surprise.

PAINT A FACE

Dad's Day Dessert Tie

June

Serves 2 to 4

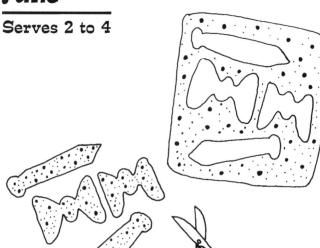

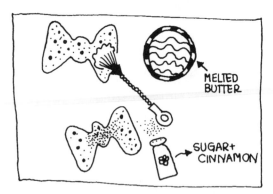

MELTED BUTTER

SUGAR + CINNAMON

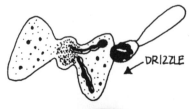

DRIZZLE

Ingredients

flour tortillas, large burrito size, 1 per person
melted butter
2 teaspoons sugar
2 tablespoons milk

2 teaspoons cinnamon
¼ cup chocolate chips
6 caramels

Utensils

oven preheated to 400°F
scissors
empty salt shaker
oven mitt
microwave-safe bowl or saucepan

marker and paper
pastry brush
baking sheet
measuring spoons
spoons

Process

1. Draw a large, simple bow tie with the marker on the sheet of paper to make a pattern. Cut the bow tie pattern out with scissors. Place the pattern on the flour tortilla.
2. Cut around the tortilla with a knife or kitchen scissors to make a bow tie shape. Make as many bow ties on flour tortillas as desired. Experiment with making two regular long tie shapes, too, facing opposite directions on the tortilla. See illustration.
3. Dip the pastry brush into the butter and brush butter on the ties. Put the cinnamon and sugar in a salt shaker. Shake the mixed sugar and cinnamon on the buttery tortilla ties. Then, slip the ties on the baking sheet.
4. Put the tortilla ties in the oven and bake for 5 to 8 minutes or until the sugar and cinnamon are nicely browned and bubbly. Wear an oven mitt and remove the hot tortilla ties from the oven. Set aside.
5. Place the chocolate chips and 1 tablespoon of milk in a microwave-safe bowl and mix with a spoon. Then, microwave the chips and milk on medium heat until melted. Mix the caramels and 1 tablespoon of milk in a bowl and microwave on medium until melted. The chocolate chips and caramels can also be melted in a saucepan.
6. To decorate the bow ties, dip a spoon in the melted chocolate and then in melted caramel. Drizzle the chocolate and caramel over the bow ties.
7. Put the bow ties on a serving plate and surprise Dad or any other hungry folks. It might be fun to serve the crunchy, sweet ties in a wrapped tie box like a gift for dad to open.

Frozen Juice Cubes

beverage   10 to 15 minutes   easiest

Ingredients

favorite summer beverage(s), such as
    fruit juice   lemonade
    fruit drink   sparkling juices
maraschino or mint cherry, one for each glass
thin slices of favorite citrus fruit(s), such as
    lime   orange
    grapefruit   lemon
water or other summer drink
optional drink garnishes, such as
    fruit kabob on a toothpick
    nontoxic flower
    paper umbrella

Utensils

ice cube trays
tall, cold glasses
straw or swizzle stick, optional

Process

1. Fill one ice cube tray with a summer beverage or juice.
2. Place one cherry in each section of another ice cube tray and add water.
3. Place both trays in the freezer until solid.
4. Chill fruits in the refrigerator.
5. Serve a favorite summer drink or ice water with the colored ice cubes, cherry ice cubes and thin fruits floating in the drink or perched on the rim of the glass.
6. Add a straw, a swizzle stick, a fruit kabob, paper umbrella or a flower to make the beverage even fancier, if desired.

▲ Serve with a spoon to avoid choking hazards.

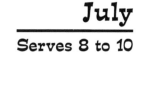

July

Serves 8 to 10

Firecracker Sandwiches

July

Serves 8

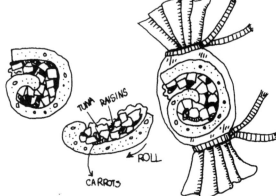

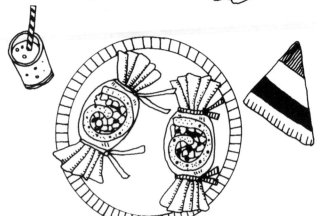

Ingredients

1 13-ounce can chunk light tuna packed in water, drained

⅓ cup mayonnaise

1 medium-size carrot, peeled and grated

8 slices firm white bread with crusts removed

¼ teaspoon salt

¼ cup dark raisins

lemonade, optional

Utensils

mixing bowl and spoon

colored plastic wrap

rolling pin

twist-ties or colorful ribbons

Process

1. Place the tuna, mayonnaise and salt in the bowl and mix well with a spoon.
2. Add the grated carrot to the tuna mixture and mix in.
3. Stir the raisins into the tuna mixture and mix again. Set aside.
4. Place one slice of bread on a work surface and flatten it with a rolling pin into a thin, flat piece.
5. Spread ¼ cup or less tuna mixture evenly on the flattened slice of bread.
6. Roll up the bread with tuna mixture, jelly-roll fashion. Set aside on the work surface.
7. Continue flattening and filling more bread with the tuna mixture and rolling into jelly rolls. Set all the sandwiches aside as they are completed.
8. Wrap each rolled sandwich in colored plastic wrap, twisting ends with twist-ties or colorful ribbons to resemble firecrackers.
9. Put the firecracker sandwiches on a plate or stack them in a basket to serve for a 4th of July party appetizer or lunch. Serve with ice-cold lemonade in a tall glass with red, white and blue paper napkins to brighten a happy day.

Flag Toast

Ingredients

1 slice of bread, crust removed
1 tablespoon cream cheese, softened
12 raisins
2 teaspoons jam
optional fruits or veggies for flag decoration, such as

peas	olives	berries
bananas	chopped apple	currants
golden raisins		

Utensils

butter knife
cake decorator
chop stick
▲ A clean mustard or ketchup squeeze bottle works in place of a
cake decorator, if preferred. Also, a plastic sandwich bag with one little
corner snipped off for the decorating point works well too. (See page 146.)

Process

1. Place the bread in the toaster and toast just until the bread hardens. Do not brown the bread.
2. Spread the cream cheese on one side of the toast with a butter knife. Set aside.
3. Spoon jam into the cake decorator, squeeze bottle or plastic bag.
4. Squeeze stripes and designs onto the toast to resemble a flag. Flags can be of this country, other countries, or design a flag from an imaginary country, planet, club or world.
5. Decorate the toast with raisins for stars or other foods of any kind.
6. Position the flag toast on the plate.
7. Place the chop stick to the left of the flag, to represent the flag pole, and serve.

July

Allow 1 flag per person

CREAM CHEESE

SPOON IN JAM

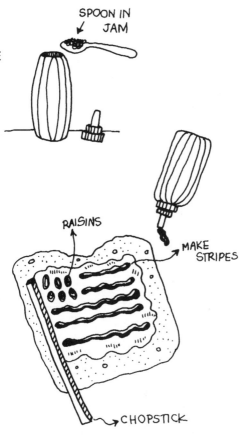

RAISINS

MAKE STRIPES

CHOPSTICK

easier

about 45 minutes

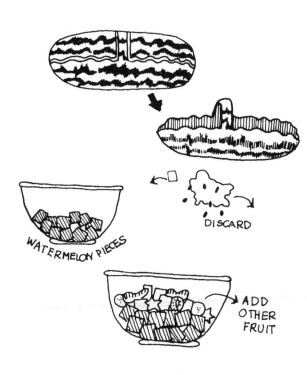
fruit

Summer Fruit Basket

August

Serves 4 to 12 — depending on the size of the watermelon

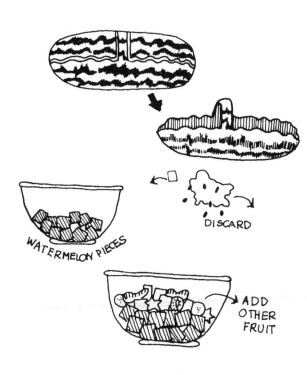

WATERMELON PIECES

DISCARD

ADD OTHER FRUIT

Ingredient

ripe watermelon
any selection of ripe, tropical style fruits, such as

melons	pineapple	kiwi
strawberries	orange sections	bananas
mango	papaya	star fruit

shredded coconut, optional

Utensils

bamboo skewer	paring knife	kitchen towel
big spoon	cutting board	bowl
paper towels		

Process

1. Use a bamboo skewer or the point of the knife to score a basic basket shape with a handle on the watermelon. Cut on the scored line with a paring knife — like carving a pumpkin — to cut away the watermelon that is not part of the basket design. See illustration.
▲ This line can be cut straight, wiggly, scalloped, or in any other design. Keep the handle fairly wide and thick so it will be strong. Be careful of slippery, sticky hands. Keep a towel handy to wipe knife and keep hands dry.
2. Scoop out all the pink, juicy watermelon and place it on the cutting board. Cut away any rind or seeds of the watermelon that are left.
3. Cut this watermelon into chunks and place chunks in the bowl.
4. Next, cut the other fruits into chunks, balls, slices or shapes and place them in the bowl with the watermelon. Let them sit while the juices and flavors mix.
5. Pat the inside of the watermelon "basket" dry with paper towels.
6. Scoop the fruit salad into the "basket," heaping it high above the sides of the basket. Sprinkle coconut on the top, if desired.
7. Set the basket of summer fruits on the table for a bright, juicy, refreshing fruit salad in its own basket, ideal for a buffet, party or picnic.

Tomato Summer Sandwiches

sandwich

bake

about 30 minutes

easiest

August

Allow 2 flowers per person

Ingredients

medium ripe tomatoes
2 slices whole wheat bread per person
2 slices low-fat cheese per person

Utensils

oven preheated to 350°F
cookie cutter, flower shape

knife and cutting board
cookie sheet

Process

1. Slice the ripe tomato into thin slices. One medium tomato should yield about four to six slices. Set aside.
2. Place a piece of bread on the cutting board and top with one slice of cheese.
3. Press a flower-shaped cookie cutter into the bread and cheese. Save the scraps for nibbling while cooking.
4. Place the bread and cheese flower on the cookie sheet.
5. Continue cutting out bread and cheese for as many people as necessary, counting two slices of bread and cheese for each person. Place them on the cookie sheet.
6. Place the cookie sheet in the oven and heat until the cheese bubbles and melts, usually 2 to 4 minutes.
7. Remove the cookie sheet to the cutting board. Place one tomato slice on each sandwich. Return to the oven briefly to heat through.
8. Remove again. Serve warm or cool.

TOMATO

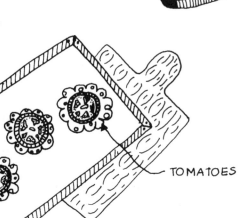

TOMATOES

Back-to-School Cookies

September

Serves approximately 8 hands — depending on child's hand size

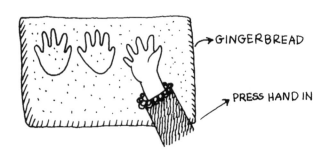

→ GINGERBREAD

→ PRESS HAND IN

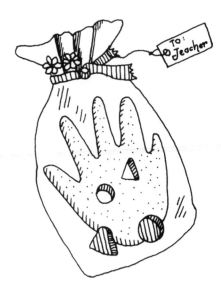

TO: Teacher

Ingredients

nonstick cooking spray
1 box gingerbread cake mix with cookie directions (or use gingerbread cookie recipe on page 148)
flour

Utensils

oven preheated to 350°F or as directed on the gingerbread mix box

baking sheet	rolling pin
knife	spatula
tiny cookie cutters	wax paper
clear plastic wrap	ribbon
oven mitt	

Process

1. Spray a light coating of cooking spray on the surface of the baking sheet. Set aside.
2. Follow the directions on the box to prepare the gingerbread cookies.
3. Roll out the dough on a floured surface. Place one hand on the rolled out gingerbread dough and press into the dough to make a clear, indented impression.
4. Cut around the outline of the handprint with a knife. Make several more handprints until the dough is used. Form the scraps into little shapes and cookies for fun, too.
5. Carefully lift each gingerbread handprint with a spatula and hands, and place it on the baking sheet. Do the same for extra cookies or shapes.
6. If desired, cut designs in the handprint with the tiny cookie cutters. Bake these shapes, too.
7. Place the baking sheet with gingerbread cookies in the oven and bake according to package directions, usually about 6 to 8 minutes.
8. Wear an oven mitt to remove the handprints and cookies from the oven. Cool briefly. Transfer the handprints and cookies from the baking sheet with a spatula to wax paper.
9. Wrap each handprint in clear plastic wrap and tie with a ribbon. Tuck the little cookies or shapes into the handprint gift, if desired, or eat while wrapping the handprints. Give the wrapped cookies to favorite teachers, special relatives or kind neighbors.

Apple for My Teacher

Ingredients

1 package frozen puff pastry
1 tablespoon lemon juice
¼ teaspoon cinnamon

Golden Delicious apples
1 teaspoon sugar

Utensils

oven preheated to 375°F or according to package directions

apple corer
small bowl and spoon
baking sheet
spatula

knife and cutting board
measuring spoons
oven mitt

Process

1. Open the package of puff pastry and remove one sheet of pastry dough to thaw.
2. While waiting, core the apples with the apple corer and slice into small pieces with a knife. Place the apple pieces in a small bowl. Sprinkle them with the lemon juice and toss lightly with the spoon to cover apples with lemon juice.
3. Add the cinnamon and sugar to the apple slices and toss well with the spoon.
4. Cut about a 4 to 8-inch square from the pastry dough. Place the dough on the work surface.
5. Form the dough into a flat shape, such as an apple, a schoolhouse, a book or any other symbol having to do with school. Form the shape so it has sides on it. See the illustration.
6. Place the pastry shape on the baking sheet. Spoon some of the apple mixture on the pastry. Follow the same procedure in molding the remaining dough into school symbols or other designs and place on the baking sheet.
7. When all of the dough is used, place the apple and pastry shapes in the oven. Bake until the pastry turns golden brown, approximately 4 to 6 minutes.
8. Wear an oven mitt and remove the apple pastries from the oven. Let cool for a few minutes. Then, remove the pastries with a spatula.
9. Place one or all of the pastries in a box lined with wax paper and give to a teacher. Keep a few to share with the family

September

Allow 1 apple per person

A Year Full of Special Days

Dried Apple Chain

October

Serves Many

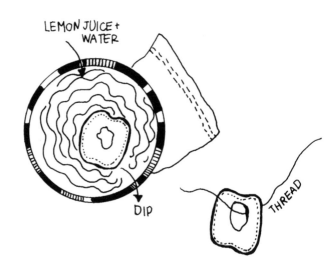

LEMON JUICE + WATER

DIP

THREAD

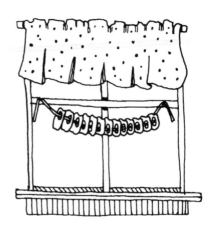

Ingredients

1 cup lemon juice
3 cups water
apples

Utensils

small bowl and spoon
knife and cutting board
sturdy thread

apple peeler and corer
paper towels
ribbon, optional

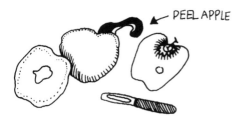

PEEL APPLE

Process

1. Mix the lemon juice and water in a small bowl.
2. Peel and core as many apples as desired with the apple peeler. Slice apples in ⅓ inch thick rings with a knife.
3. Dip each apple ring into the lemon juice and water mixture to prevent browning. Then, pat dry with a paper towel.
4. String a piece of sturdy thread through the center of each ring.
5. Hang the string of apples in a dry, warm place — near a wood stove or sunny window is ideal. The rings will take approximately one to two weeks to dry, depending on the room conditions.
6. Periodically taste test an apple ring to determine if the apples are dry enough. Dry rings will have a chewy, almost leathery texture and almost no juice.
7. When apple rings are completely dried, hang them in a place where they can be snacked on and enjoyed.
8. Add ribbon to hang the apple rings in a decorative way.
▲ To speed up the drying process, dry the apples in a warm oven. Place the slices (not on a string) on a wire cooling rack placed on a baking sheet so the air can circulate. Place the sheet in a 150°F oven for about four hours, turning apples once. Remove when fully dried. They may be eaten immediately or cooled before placing in a jar to store.

Halloween Cheese Ball

snack   about 30 minutes   easy

Ingredients

2 cups (8 ounces) shredded cheddar cheese
¼ cup solid-pack canned pumpkin
¼ teaspoon allspice
one-half of a large pretzel stick
any selection of favorite foods for decorations, such as
    red or green bell peppers
    parsley sprigs
    carrot sticks or circles
assorted crackers

1 (4 ounce) package cream cheese, softened
¼ cup pineapple preserves
¼ teaspoon ground nutmeg

    black olive slices
    celery slices
    spinach leaves

October

Serves 4 to 8

Utensils

measuring cups
electric mixer
butter knife or spreading knife

mixing bowl
plastic wrap

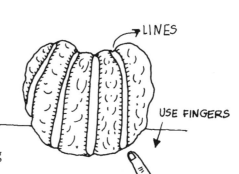

Process

1. Place the cheddar cheese, cream cheese, pumpkin, pineapple preserves and spices in a medium bowl.
2. With an electric mixer, beat the mixture until smooth, starting on low speed, then increasing speed as mixture smoothes.
3. Cover the bowl with plastic wrap and refrigerate 2 to 3 hours to chill and firm.
4. When chilled and firm, remove the pumpkin-cheese mixture from the bowl and place it on a plate. Using hands, shape the mixture into a round pumpkin or ball.
5. Shape the top of the ball inward to resemble the top of a pumpkin. With fingers, score vertical lines down the pumpkin's sides. See the illustration.
6. Place the pretzel rod in top for a stem. Use food to decorate the pumpkin and add facial features.
7. Surround the pumpkin with crackers. Add a butter knife or spreading knife and serve the appetizer jack-o-lantern with crackers for a party treat or snack.

easy

1 hour or more

snack

Lantern Light Snack

October

Serves 2 to 4 — depending on the size of the pumpkin

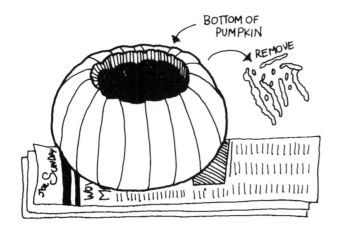

BOTTOM OF PUMPKIN

REMOVE

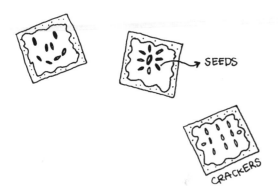

SEEDS

CRACKERS

Ingredients

nonstick cooking spray
salt, optional
peanut butter
variety of edible seeds, such as

sesame	poppy
sunflower	pumpkin

small pumpkin
crackers

Utensils

glass baking dish
knife
large bowl
apple corer, melon ball scoop
metal pie plate

newspapers
spoon or scoop
paper towels
votive candle

Process

The seeds

1. Spray the glass dish with nonstick cooking spray. Set aside.
2. Set the pumpkin on a triple layer of newspaper on the floor.
3. Cut a hole about the size of a closed fist in the bottom of the pumpkin with a knife. Lift out the cut-out piece of pumpkin and add to the compost.
4. Scoop out the seeds and stringy fibers from the pumpkin by spoon and by hand.
5. Place the seeds in a large bowl of water and rinse them to remove the attached strings and fibers. Add the strings to the compost pile, too.
6. Let the seeds dry on paper towels. Pat them with more towels to speed the process.
7. When dry, spread the seeds out in the glass dish and microwave on high for 5 to 6 minutes, stirring at the end of each minute, or cook in the oven. Cook until the seeds are crispy, then cool slightly. Add some salt to the seeds, if desired.
8. While the seeds cool, spread peanut butter on crackers.
9. Then, create designs, faces and features on the crackers with any of the seeds. Set aside on wax paper.

The lantern

1. Remove any remaining fibers or pulp so that the pumpkin is completely scraped clean inside. Add the pulp to the compost pile.
2. Dry the pumpkin with a paper towel, inside and out, to help prevent slippery surfaces.
3. Poke holes in the pumpkin with the apple corer in any pattern or design. Carefully use other tools such as a melon ball scoop or knife to add further designs.
▲ It is not always necessary to cut all the way through the pumpkin. Carving, etching or scraping the skin away adds creative design too. Try to keep hands and tools wiped dry to prevent slippery fingers.

To light the lantern

1. Place the candle in the center of the pie plate.
2. Light the candle and place the pumpkin lantern over it. To serve, arrange the decorated crackers around the jack-o-lantern. Turn out the lights and tell scary stories while munching the spooky treats by lantern light.
3. When done, blow out the candle and turn on the lights.

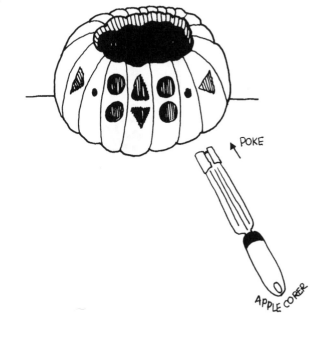

easiest   10 to 15 minutes   beverage

Hot Chocolate Muggies

November

Makes many special gift packets

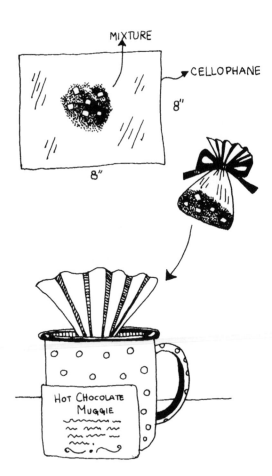

MIXTURE

CELLOPHANE

8"

8"

HOT CHOCOLATE
MUGGIE

Ingredients

2¾ cups of nonfat dry milk
1¼ cup of sugar

1½ cups cocoa
1 bag small marshmallows

Utensils

bowl and spoon
scissors
ribbon

colored cellophane or plastic wrap
teaspoon
1 or more decorative mugs, optional

Process

1. Place all of the ingredients in the bowl and mix with the spoon.
2. Cut a piece of cellophane or plastic wrap about 8 by 8 inches.
3. Place 4 teaspoons of the mixture in the center of the cellophane or plastic wrap square for an individual serving, or the entire mixture for several servings.
4. Gather the corners of the cellophane or plastic wrap and bunch at the top.
5. Tie the ribbon with a tight knot at the top. Then, make a bow.
6. Place the individual mixture in the mug.
7. Print these recipe directions on a card:

> **Hot Chocolate Muggie**
> Place this mixture in your mug and add 2 tablespoons of milk. Mix until smooth. Stir in 1½ cups hot milk. Drink and enjoy.

8. Make 1 or several packets for each mug.
▲ Give mugs as a gift with the Hot Chocolate Muggie Mix, if desired.

Mini-Pastry Cornucopia

vegetable   bake   1 hour or more   easy

Ingredients

nonstick cooking spray

1 cup water

choice of small fresh vegetables, such as
   corn, green peas, cherry tomatoes

choice of fresh vegetables cut very small, such as
   green beans, carrots, cauliflower, broccoli, celery

refrigerator puff pastry dough

1 egg

November

Each sheet of puff pastry dough makes 4 cornucopias

Utensils

oven preheated to 375°F or as directed on the package

baking sheet	small bowl	cone-shaped paper cups
whisk	pastry brush	oven mitt
spatula	knife and cutting board	

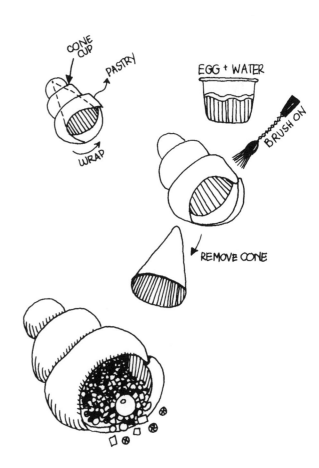

Process

1. Spray a light coating of cooking spray on the baking sheet and also spray a coating of cooking spray on the outside of the cone-shaped paper cups. Set aside.

2. Cut the pastry dough into strips about ¼-inch wide. Beginning at the point of the cup, wrap the pastry dough around and around the cup. Overlap the dough to resemble a cornucopia. See illustration.

3. Wet the end of the dough with a little water and press so it sticks together to end the design. This will form a cone or cornucopia shape.

4. Break the egg over a bowl. Add the water and whisk. Set aside briefly.

5. Carefully place the pastry cornucopias (still on the paper cups) onto the baking sheet.

6. Dip the pastry brush into the egg and water mixture and brush the outside of the pastry cornucopias to add a glaze.

7. Place the cornucopias in the oven and bake for 10 minutes. Wear an oven mitt and remove the cornucopias from the oven. Transfer the cornucopias from the baking sheet to a platter with the spatula. Cool completely.

8. Remove the paper cups. Arrange the miniature cut vegetable pieces inside each cornucopia.

9. Serve the little cornucopias as an accompaniment to a main meal or as a tasty, creative vegetable snack or party food.

Chocolate Spoons

November

Recipe makes approximately 20 spoons — allow 1 spoon per person

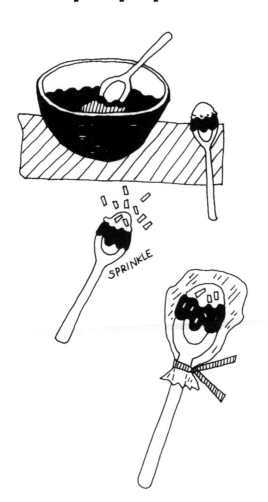

SPRINKLE

Ingredients
1 package chocolate chips
1 package butterscotch chips
sugar sprinkles, optional

Utensils
2 saucepans or microwave-safe bowls
small wooden or plastic spoons, any color
ribbon

wooden mixing spoons
plastic wrap or colored cellophane

Process
1. Place the chocolate chips in a saucepan or small microwave-safe bowl.
2. Microwave the chocolate chips on medium for 2 minutes and then stir with the mixing spoon. Let stand about 1 minute, then stir again until smooth.
3. Place the butterscotch chips in another bowl.
4. Repeat the procedure with the butterscotch chips — microwave on medium for 2 minutes and then stir. Let stand about 1 minute, then stir again until smooth. The chocolate chips and butterscotch chips can also be melted in a saucepan on the stove.
5. To decorate each spoon, dip one end into either the melted chocolate or the melted butterscotch, or dip a spoon deep into the chocolate, let it set briefly, then dip just the tip of the spoon into the butterscotch, layering the two flavors. Experiment with dipping patterns.
6. Before the dipped chocolate or butterscotch dries, sprinkle sugar onto the dipped ends of the spoons, if desired.
7. Place the spoon on plastic wrap and dry.
8. Wrap each spoon in cellophane or plastic wrap. Tie a piece of ribbon around the spoon to hold the cellophane in place.
▲ Give several spoons as a gift for someone special to enjoy with hot chocolate or coffee or to eat like a lollipop. Makes a great gift when combined with Hot Chocolate Muggies, page 172.

Noodle Wreath

entree   about 45 minutes   easier

Ingredients

December
Serves 4 to 8

nonstick cooking spray
2 (12-ounce) packages of uncooked spinach fettucine
prepared meatballs, optional
large jar of pasta sauce (or favorite spaghetti sauce recipe)
Parmesan cheese
spinach leaves, optional

Utensils

10-inch ring mold pan	saucepan
mixing spoon	water
large plate	strainer

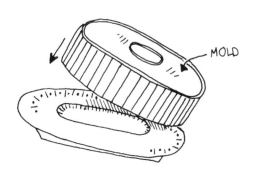

Process

1. Spray the ring mold with cooking spray. Set aside.
2. Cook the fettucine in a saucepan over medium high heat until soft but not mushy. Drain the fettucine noodles but do not rinse.
3. Pack the fettucine in the ring mold by pressing firmly into the mold with the back of a smooth spoon. Cool in the refrigerator.
4. To unmold, put a plate on top of the mold. Then, hold the mold and the plate together with two hands and carefully and quickly flip the plate so the fettucine mold releases from the pan into the plate.
5. Arrange the meatballs around the fettucine wreath, if desired.
6. Heat the sauce in a saucepan or in a microwave-safe bowl covered with wax paper for several minutes until warmed through. Pour the sauce over the fettucine wreath. Cover the wreath with a sheet of wax paper. Place it in the microwave for 3 minutes on medium, or in the oven, until heated through.
7. Tuck some spinach leaves around the wreath for holiday coloring and sprinkle with Parmesan cheese to resemble snow or sparkles.
8. Serve as a festive holiday dinner.

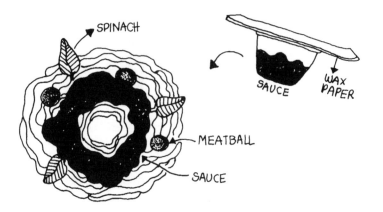

Holiday Tortilla Tree

December

One-half pound of ground beef (or turkey or chicken) makes about 6 tortillas

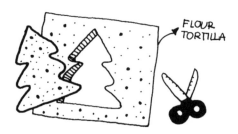

FLOUR TORTILLA

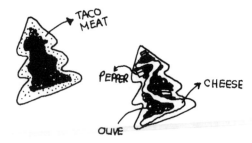

TACO MEAT
PEPPER
CHEESE
OLIVE

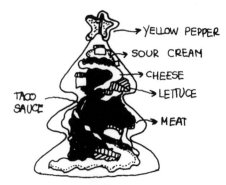

YELLOW PEPPER
SOUR CREAM
CHEESE
LETTUCE
MEAT
TACO SAUCE

Ingredients

½ pound ground beef (or turkey or chicken)
6 large flour tortillas
1 red bell pepper, seeded and diced
¼ cup sliced black olives
6 ounces any yellow cheese, cut into strips
3 cups shredded lettuce
taco sauce

1 package taco seasoning mix
1 green bell pepper, seeded and diced
1 tomato, diced
⅛ cup sliced green olives
yellow pepper
sour cream

Utensils

oven preheated to 350°F
wooden spoon
baking sheet
oven mitt

frying pan
kitchen scissors
knife and cutting board
spatula

Process

1. Brown the ground beef in a frying pan over medium heat, stirring with a wooden spoon until the beef is dry and crumbly. Mix the ground beef and taco mix according to the taco mix package directions. Cook as directed and then set aside.
2. Cut large flour tortillas into tree shapes with kitchen scissors. Give the scraps to the birds and outdoor critters, or nibble while cooking.
3. Place the tortilla trees on the baking sheet. With a spoon, spread a very thin layer of the taco meat evenly over each tortilla tree. Leave a ½-inch border of tortilla all the way around each tree.
4. Use green peppers, tomato and olives to decorate the tortillas like Christmas trees. Arrange the cheese on each tortilla in a zigzag pattern to make a garland or other festive design.
5. Then, bake the trees in the oven for 5 to 7 minutes or until the cheese is melted.
6. Meanwhile, clean a yellow pepper and cut it in half. Set it aside until just before serving.
7. Wear an oven mitt and remove the tortilla trees from the oven. With the spatula, transfer the tortillas from the baking sheet to individual plates.
8. Decorate each tortilla tree with lettuce, sour cream and drizzles of taco sauce.
9. To complete each tree design, cut a freehand designed star for each tree out of the yellow pepper with a knife or kitchen scissors. Place a star at the top of each tortilla tree and serve for a special holiday lunch or dinner.

Heavenly Carrot Stars

Ingredients

large, fat carrots

Utensils

vegetable peeler
knife and cutting board
citrus stripper

Process

1. Scrape a carrot with the vegetable peeler. Discard peelings.
2. Place the carrot on the cutting board.
3. Cut off the stem of the carrot. Cut off any part of the carrot that is not ½ inch in diameter and save these remaining parts or eat them as a snack.
4. Hold the carrot upright, resting on the wide flat end.
5. Use a citrus stripper to cut a thin lengthwise slice from one side of the carrot.
6. Turn the carrot a little. Hold the carrot on the wide flat end as in step 4 and repeat the thin slicing with the citrus stripper, making a second cut.
7. Continue steps 5 and 6 until a total of 5 cuts have been made. (Any number of cuts makes a design but 5 makes the traditional star shape.)
8. Place the carrot on its side. Slice the carrot to make stars.
9. Eat the stars for a raw vegetable snack, for dipping or for a garnish in salads or other recipes.

December

Serves 1 or more

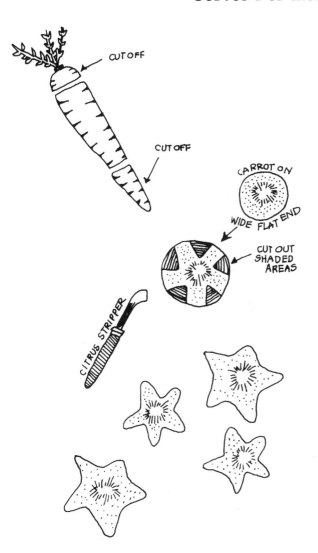

CUT OFF

CUT OFF

CARROT ON WIDE FLAT END

CUT OUT SHADED AREAS

CITRUS STRIPPER

Spinning Dreidels

December

Serves 8 to 10

Ingredients

1 bag of chocolate candy kisses
1 small jar of smooth peanut butter
1 bag of large marshmallows
1 bag of thin pretzel sticks

Utensils

butter knife

Process

1. Take the wrappings off the chocolate kisses.
2. Spread about a teaspoon of peanut butter on the flat bottom of one of the kisses.
3. Press the flat bottom of a marshmallow on the peanut buttered side of the candy kiss.
4. Poke a pretzel stick through the end of the marshmallow opposite the candy kiss, pressing until the pretzel stick just touches the candy kiss.
5. Hold the end of the pretzel stick to twist and spin this yummy dessert that looks like a dreidel.
6. Eat in celebration of Chanukah.

New Year's Eve Cracker Snackers

December

Serves many excited celebrators

Ingredients

bite-size crackers, cereals, nuts, dried fruit or other snacks, such as

fish-shaped crackers

raisins

popcorn

pretzel bits

chocolate chips

Utensils

wax paper

tape

tissue paper, especially in bright colors

stickers or name tags, optional

sandwich bags

toilet paper tubes, one for each cracker snacker

ribbon or rubber bands

basket or bowl

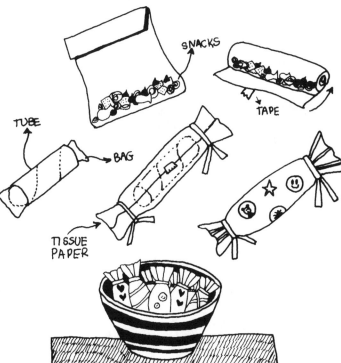

Process

1. Spread out the selected crackers, cereals and other bite-size snacks on a sheet of wax paper. Mix the snacks together by hand.
2. Scoop up a handful, about ½ cup, of the mixed snacks and put them in a plastic sandwich bag. Let the snacks settle across the bottom in the bag. Then, roll the bag into a hot dog-shaped tube, starting at the snack end of the bag. Secure with a little piece of tape to keep the roll in shape.
3. Slip the rolled tube into a cardboard toilet paper tube.
4. Wrap the toilet paper tube with tissue paper, letting extra tissue stick out at both ends of the tube. Tape the tissue paper at the center of the tube.
5. Next, gather the tissue at the ends and tie with ribbon or rubber bands.
6. Decorate the tube with stickers or a name tag or more ribbons. This is the Cracker Snacker. Create as many Cracker Snackers as needed.
7. Fill a basket or bowl with the fluffy tissue paper ends of the Cracker Snackers showing.
8. On New Year's Eve after the stroke of midnight and after all the banging of pans and sounding of horns, each person can tear open a Cracker Snacker and enjoy the yummy contents.

Because young children may not stay up until midnight, stage a pretend New Year's Eve at a convenient time. Keep in mind that most children enjoy the celebration more when it is very dark outside and seems just like midnight!

Flavored Gift Oil

December

Each bottle or jar makes one gift

ONION

GARLIC

PEPPER

SKEWER

To You
A gift!

Ingredients

olive oil
green bell pepper
pearl onions
choice of herbs, such as

basil
parsley, dry or sprig
mint, dry or sprig
chives
sorrel

red bell pepper
garlic cloves

dill weed, dry or sprig
oregano
thyme
rosemary

Utensils

small sieve
knife and cutting board
ribbon
pens or crayons to decorate label or card

decorative bottle or jar with lid
long bamboo skewer (no taller than bottle)
plain stick-on label or small gift card

Process

1. Place the sieve in the top of the bottle. Pour the olive oil into the bottle.
2. Cut off the tops of the bell peppers. Clean and core the peppers. Cut into small pieces.
3. Make a decorative skewer by assembling the onions, bell peppers and garlic cloves in a creative design or sequence.
4. Slip the skewer into the bottle. (If the skewer is too long, snip with scissors or break by hand.) If desired, place several sprigs of one of the herbs in the bottle, too.
5. Tighten the lid on the bottle. Tie a bow around the neck of the bottle.
6. Add a hand-decorated label or gift card to the bottle and give the flavored bottle of olive oil as a gift to someone who loves to cook or make salad dressings from scratch.

▲ This flavored recipe also works with vinegar instead of olive oil. Consider other flavorings, herbs or spices.

Indexes

Index of Terms

Cooking Art

Index by food category

Beverage

Bread

Breakfast

Condiment

Craft

Dessert

Entree

Fruit

Pet food

Salad

Sandwich

Projects requiring the use of an oven

Projects requiring no baking

(May require cooking, heating or freezing)

Common U.S. Measurements and Metric Equivalents

Recipes in this book have been written and tested using standard U.S. measurements. Metric conversions given here are approximate.

Volume

1/8 cup – 30mL
1/4 cup – 60 mL
1/3 cup – 75 mL
1/2 cup (4 oz.) – 125 mL
2/3 cup – 150 mL
3/4 cup – 175 mL
1 cup (8 oz.) – 250 mL
2 cups – 500 mL
1 pint (16 oz.) – 500 mL (.5 L)
1 quart – 1 L
1 gallon – 4 L
1/8 teaspoon – .5 mL
1/4 teaspoon – 1 mL
1/2 teaspoon – 2.5 mL
3/4 teaspoon – 3.5 mL
1 teaspoon – 5 mL
1 1/2 teaspoon – 7.5 mL
1 Tablespoon – 15 mL
2 Tablespoons (1 ounce) – 30 mL

Weight

1/2 ounce – 15 grams
1 ounce – 30 grams
4 ounces (1/4 pound) – 110 grams
8 ounces (1/2 pound) – 225 grams
16 ounces (1 pound) – 450 grams

Temperatures

32°F (water freezes) – 0°C
212°F (water boils) – 100°C
275°F – 140°C
300°F (slow oven) – 150°C
325°F – 160°C
350°F (moderate oven) – 180°C
375°F – 190°C
400°F (hot oven) – 200°C
425°F – 220°C
450°F (very hot oven) – 230°C

Inches

1/8 – 3 mm
1/4 – 6 mm
1/2 – 13 mm
3/4 – 19 mm
1 – 2.5 cm
2 – 5 cm
12 (1 foot) – 30 cm